Praise for *Middle Leaders*

CW00644343

Adam Robbins' book is a .... ice o................... a school setting. Whereas most leadership books are full of g......... approac..... egies, this book is concrete, detailed and supported by a wealth of both experience and evidence. Whether you are looking for an explainer to assessment theory, a primer for budgeting and running meetings, or even psychological advice on staying motivated in a tremendously challenging role, this book has it all.

Adam Boxer, Head of Science, The Totteridge Academy

In writing *Middle Leadership Mastery*, Adam Robbins has produced a book for secondary school middle leaders who want to be authentic in their challenging role. It is not for anyone who is content to simply go through the motions. On the contrary, it is a book that might challenge your thinking as it raises important issues and sets them against key questions relating to middle leadership issues. Alongside this, Adam provides useful tools – and middle leaders will find things like the questions for effective book-looks and the drop-in proforma both pragmatic and appropriate. The structure of CPD insights will also be welcomed by anyone who is responsible for this area.

Bill Lowe, middle leadership specialist, researcher and author

Middle Leadership Mastery provides carefully considered, thoroughly researched and referenced advice for subject leaders, and also considers pastoral responsibilities in addition to academic ones. It draws together much recent research and helpful reading, focusing on what middle leaders can learn from the findings – which, in turn, should help enable them to lead their teams effectively.

Dr Jill Berry, leadership development consultant and author of *Making the Leap: Moving from Deputy to Head*

Middle Leadership Mastery will certainly be a useful addition to the armoury of any middle leader in the education sector, and I would also see a place for this book as a course reader for final-year undergraduate trainees on initial teacher education (ITE) courses – and indeed on my own PGCE course.

Mark Chidler, Primary PGCE Course Coordinator, Newman University Birmingham

Adam Robbins clearly identifies how middle leaders can harness the responsibilities and freedom of the education system in terms of teaching, learning and assessment. And, by drawing upon key underpinnings of the new Ofsted framework, he shares various perspectives geared towards questioning and challenging existing classroom practice. Robbins presents a range of resources for managing key areas of education and explicitly identifies how to tackle some of the difficult challenges of being a leader, from time management to delegation. Throughout the book, there are a wealth of opportunities to explore and reflect upon this newfound knowledge, which will ultimately impact upon the children and the curriculum within our schools. Undeniably, Robbins' honest account of his experiences of leadership shine through, developing the relatability of the book's content to the everyday classroom.

Jenny Wilkinson, teacher and middle leader, Church of the Ascension Primary School

We all know that the individual teacher makes more difference to pupil outcomes however good or bad the school is. Beyond that, the phase leader or head of department cultivates the climate in which the teacher can create good classroom weather on a daily basis. Adam Robbins' *Middle Leadership Mastery* is a book to help that process. Every primary school and every secondary school department should have a copy, and discussion of the approaches contained with it at staff meetings will help teachers create good classroom weather even on a rainy day or when the wind blows.

Tim Brighouse, former London Schools Commissioner and Chief Education Officer for Birmingham and Oxfordshire

Middle Leadership Mastery is first class and an excellent contribution to the school leadership literature. It is packed with a wealth of relevant research and insights, and is brought to life through Robbins' honesty and humility in relating his first-hand experiences of teaching and leading. The work of middle leaders in schools is complex and challenging – and *Middle Leadership Mastery* is ambitious in its aim to codify the knowledge and expertise of school leaders, which are often crowded out in a discourse dominated by tales of heroism and the cult of personality.

Tom Rees, Executive Director, Ambition Institute, and former head teacher

It's often said that middle leaders are the engine room of a great school: their energy, their effectiveness and their commitment are vital to any school's success. In writing this book, Adam Robbins has used his extensive knowledge to produce a superb and impressively comprehensive guide – covering curriculum design, assessment, teacher development and more besides – for anyone undertaking one of these all-important roles.

Tom Sherrington, education consultant and author of *Teaching WalkThrus*

Adam Robbins

Middle Leadership
Mastery

A toolkit for subject and pastoral leaders

Crown House Publishing Limited
www.crownhouse.co.uk

First published by
Crown House Publishing Limited
Crown Buildings, Bancyfelin, Carmarthen, Wales, SA33 5ND, UK
www.crownhouse.co.uk

and

Crown House Publishing Company LLC
PO Box 2223, Williston, VT 05495, USA
www.crownhousepublishing.com

First published 2021. Reprinted 2021 (twice).

Cover image © tadamichi – stock.adobe.com.

Tea cup image, page 7 © lyudinka – stock.adobe.com. Car image, page 8 © Comauthor – stock.adobe.com.

Extract page 59 and figure page 60 © Robert Coe, 2018. From Why Assessment May Tell You Less Than
You Think – Part I, *CEM Blog* [blog] (21 November). Available at: https://www.cem.org/blog/
why-assessment-may-tell-you-less-than-you-think-part-1. Reproduced with permission.

British Library Cataloguing-in-Publication Data

A catalogue entry for this book is available from the British Library.

Print ISBN 978-178583534-6
Mobi ISBN 978-178583561-2
ePub ISBN 978-178583562-9
ePDF ISBN 978-178583563-6

LCCN 2021933037

Printed and bound in the UK by
Charlesworth Press, Wakefield, West Yorkshire

Acknowledgements

Firstly, I want to thank all the school leaders out there, who do an incredibly challenging job. I specifically want to thank all the leaders who I have had the chance to work with during my career: you have all taught me so much. I owe a huge debt to all those who I have worked alongside and led over the years: you too have taught me so much. I want to thank all those who I have used as references in *Middle Leadership Mastery*. I am so grateful for your insights and intellect. I specifically want to thank those who really helped me when I needed a critical friend early on in the writing process: Ruth Ashbee, Chris Baker, Matthew Benyohai, Adam Boxer, Pritesh Riachura, Kevin Robbins. I also owe a huge debt of gratitude to Sue Gerread and Deep Singh Ghataura. Deep not only checked my understanding of school assessment but also took the time to refer me to extra reading and support me with my own misconceptions as they arose. Sue was willing to give her time and expertise in cognitive science to ensure that my writing was free from error and used terminology accurately. Writing some of this book during lockdown was not an easy task, and I want to thank the proprietors of The Covid Arms for their support and encouragement every time I felt a large dose of imposter syndrome. I want to thank David Bowman and the team at Crown House Publishing for their support, feedback and professionalism in helping to create this book. I am so glad that they were willing to take a chance on me.

Finally, I would like to thank my wife, Heather, and my two daughters, Alice and Naomi. Their daily support and encouragement has helped me in ways they will never truly know.

Contents

Introduction

'You'll make a good head of department one day,' said Richard. I snorted in response and accidentally sprayed my drink across the room in disgust. I never wanted to be a leader – ever. Never wanted to get out of the classroom. Leaders were just paid more to work longer hours and do paperwork, as far as I was concerned. To be fair, to an extent, I was right. Back in the early 2000s you weren't called a middle leader; you were a coordinator of a key stage or a head of year or department. You were paid less than middle leaders currently are, but you had a mainly administrative role. Richard, a semi-retired ex-deputy who was working part-time in our department, saw through it. 'Trust me,' he replied with a wry smile. 'Sooner or later you'll do it just because you don't want someone else to screw it up!' Fast forward over a decade and I have to admit that he was right. Sadly, he died the following year, but our discussions about education and the experiences he shared have stayed with me.

During my leadership career I have made mistakes. Some of them were big; some were small. I've learnt from them, but I've also learnt from the experience of others, so hopefully I've avoided some potential pitfalls over the years. This book arises from two ideas: firstly, that there is a lot of unspoken information that middle leaders need but are not explicitly taught. Secondly, I was worried that if I didn't write it down, someone else would screw it up.

Over the last few years, schools have rightly placed a huge focus on the curriculum. This has coincided with a change in emphasis in school inspection, giving English schools much more freedom to look holistically at the choices they make for the students they serve. Alongside this there is a greater appreciation for the role of subject specialists in making decisions about the strategic direction of each department. These two issues put middle leaders in a position of great responsibility. In the last decade schools have often focused their attention on senior leadership, increasing the numbers of senior leaders and ensuring that they are able to access training and qualifications. Now it is time for middle leaders to take centre stage.

The current approach to improving the quality of middle leadership is to provide generic training with a focus on leadership styles, communicating vision and having difficult conversations. While leaders will find these skills useful in certain situations, they are only part of the toolbox needed to be successful. Tom Rees and Jen Barker of Ambition Institute believe that we require a new approach. They set out four key ideas:[1]

- **Complexity:** A leader's purpose is to improve students' learning, which is incredibly hard to do due to the complex nature of learning. This makes it hard to accurately determine the impact of leadership decisions.

- **Domain-specific expertise:** All generic leadership qualities need to be filtered through each leader's specific context. This is an often-ignored area in current training. We need to know how this expertise is developed and look beyond the surface behaviours to understand why some leaders are more successful than others.

- **Knowledge:** Leaders need to use a large array of knowledge to solve context-dependent problems in an effective manner. This knowledge is not easily acquired and covers a wide range of disciplines.

- **Persistent problems:** Leaders face a series of problems on a day-to-day basis. While each context is different, categorising the problems that persist within many school situations can allow for us to effectively share expertise.

This book aims to support these four areas from a middle leader's perspective. We discuss aspects of the complexity of school systems and their consequences. We will develop expertise by sharing stories and theories which will, in turn, increase your knowledge of pertinent aspects of middle leadership. With this knowledge you will be able to create more effective solutions to the persistent problems you face within your role.

Each chapter takes a common aspect of middle leadership and explores it in depth. By providing an overview of important concepts, illustrated by anecdotes from my ten years of leadership experience, I aim to provide a shortcut for middle leaders in all subjects and contexts. So follow me and expand your understanding.

We start with curriculum, placing that most important issue front and centre. We begin with a discussion about the value of what to teach, the skills vs knowledge debate, and how decisions will be context dependent. The chapter looks at the various stages of curriculum design before finally concluding with how best to evaluate decisions and their outcomes to inform next steps.

Chapter 2 covers teaching and learning, which can be the topic of entire books, so this chapter aims mainly to provide an overview of how our understanding of the nature of knowledge and how the brain works can support teaching. Initially, we focus on types of

---

1   T. Rees and J. Barker, 2020: A New Perspective for School Leadership? *Impact: Journal of the Chartered College of Teaching*, 9 (2020): 46–47.

knowledge and how understanding this supports explanations. This progresses into considering how students learn by providing an overview of cognitive science's understanding of the key processes involved. As the chapter develops, the emphasis shifts to developing teaching routines and introduces the concept of consistency without stifling creativity and teacher agency – a key determinant in job satisfaction.

Chapter 3 then focuses on the role of assessment. Often assessment is misunderstood; it is considered a holy tenet that it can tell you, accurately, what a student has learnt. This chapter tries to provide a counterpoint to this belief by discussing what assessment can and can't tell you before providing tangible advice on assessment in different subjects.

Chapter 4 focuses on the important role of quality-assurance metrics and their various impacts on staff morale, line management confidence and the effectiveness of the policies designed as a result of the ideas in Chapters 1 to 3.

Chapter 5 deals with a key role for many middle leaders: developing teachers. Firstly, we explore barriers to teacher development and why some commonly used strategies can backfire. Secondly, we introduce the idea of the improvement gradient and consider how learning walks and lesson visits can be used for maximum impact. Finally, we take a broad view of effective continuing professional development (CPD) and look at how this can be applied within the confines of a school's directed time budget.

Chapter 6 focuses on the brass tacks of middle leadership: decisions. This chapter looks at meeting structures and at running budgets to control costs. It pivots to discuss decision making. We explore how the best decision makers work and how to balance delegation and trust with certainty and accountability.

Chapter 7 shifts the focus to pastoral matters, beginning by examining strategies for dealing with misbehaviour in corridors and with angry parents. We explore how to build rapport and hold conversations which maintain high standards and build relationships. The chapter then covers various skills that can be deployed to support people in crisis. By introducing transactional analysis and cognitive behavioural therapy (CBT) I aim to give middle leaders the chance to be more aware of the steps they can take to support students in crisis.

The focus of Chapter 8 is on communication and people management. It is a broad-ranging chapter that starts with how people respond to change and explores moral philosophy. Once we know our decisions are based on sound rationale, we need to secure buy-in from staff. We also need to know how to manage our superiors to ensure that our decisions are not hampered by senior leadership. The chapter finishes with discussing an area that causes significant anxiety for leaders: challenging conversations. The sorts of conversations that are necessary but often difficult to have. We discuss various models to support a conversation to ensure that it is candid but dignified and developmental.

The final chapter covers many aspects of wellbeing. Its initial focus is on the personal wellbeing of the leader, using Adlerian psychology to give leaders ways of building resilience in what are often stressful situations. We discuss ways to be prepared in the event that a member of staff experiences a crisis and how we can best support them. Next, we look at what a healthy work–life balance looks like and how you can achieve it. We then explore the concept of staff wellbeing and see why token-based systems of rewards and thanks, while welcomed, are not the answer.

To a certain extent middle leadership is highly context specific. Your subject knowledge and expertise are a vital part of what makes you a good leader. There are also certain broad skills which are desirable, such as the ability to build rapport and communicate effectively. *Middle Leadership Mastery* aims to bridge the gap between those two. By introducing you to such a wide range of principles my hope is to enhance your leadership-specific knowledge base and thus support you in your role.

Each chapter ends with the opportunity to recap and reflect. This is designed to remind you of the key points covered in each chapter and support you on your mastery journey by asking you to reflect on your own experiences and context.

How to use this book

I would recommend that you start at the front and read through in order, but you can approach the chapters in any order if you want to prioritise certain areas first.

If you don't like this book, I should think it will allow a small child to get tall enough to kiss a slightly taller child, or possibly help start approximately 80 log burner fires. So, either way, it's money well spent.

Chapter 1
Leading the curriculum

No thief, however skilful, can rob one of knowledge, and that is why knowledge is the best and safest treasure to acquire.

L. Frank Baum[1]

For many years curriculum design has been in the hands of central government in each of the UK nations, not in the hands of classroom teachers. Teachers' training and planning time has focused on pedagogy and engagement. Now that all teachers have a responsibility for curriculum design, it falls to middle leaders to ensure that their curriculum is appropriately constructed and implemented. One key decision is regarding whether we build a curriculum with a foundation of knowledge or skills, as this will frame the very nature of our students' education. To make informed curriculum decisions, you need to see the big picture of education's role within society. This chapter aims to provide some of that context and offer some guidance about how to plan and implement your curriculum.

Why is the first chapter about curriculum?

Leading the curriculum is the most impactful thing that a middle leader can do. Every middle leadership role has an impact on the curriculum. Heads of subjects obviously play a role, but beneath them key stage leaders help to shape the curriculum within their areas. The curriculum is not limited to subjects taught within the school; pastoral leaders also provide a curriculum based on the work they lead with tutors, with support staff and in assemblies. The curriculum identifies the entirety of the knowledge and skills students need to acquire. This permeates through all classes and through multiple years, shaping the planning and delivery of all lessons. Your curriculum is your tool to stretch the most able and ensure all students are progressing.

---

1   L. Frank Baum, *The Lost Princess of Oz*, Project Gutenberg ebook edn (Chicago: The Reilly & Lee Co., 1917). Available at: http://www.gutenberg.org/files/24459/24459-h/24459-h.htm.

Often the power of curriculum is ignored or overlooked by middle leaders as their attention is drawn more towards operational tasks. While leaders should make time for such tasks, this is not their main purpose. Another reason why curriculum often gets pushed to the bottom of the to-do list is a perceived lack of control over it. Multi-academy trusts often stipulate a degree of control over the curriculum. Governments also stipulate what is expected nationally. While there will be some trusts with incredibly tight control of what knowledge is taught and when, the national curriculum is actually incredibly vague. For example, the Key Stage 3 guidance for history comprises a grand total of 1,242 words, most of which are non-statutory suggestions of topics.[2] So, middle leaders have a degree of flexibility regarding what is taught, when it's taught and to what depth. Even where tight external control is placed on the curriculum, you as a leader are duty-bound to ensure that it is fit for purpose in your context, make changes if necessary, and ensure that your team understands the thinking behind your decisions. At the end of the day, you are ultimately accountable to your students; they are the ones you must look in the eye on results day.

Knowledge-rich vs 21st-century skills

Over the last 50 years the curriculum has been subject to shifting priorities. The idea that skills are more important than knowledge permeated education in the 1980s.[3] Under the label of '21st-century skills', curricula shifted away from a foundation of knowledge to one of skills. More recently, some schools have been moving back towards a knowledge-rich curriculum. I first want to outline the theories behind the knowledge-rich curriculum movement to explain why it is the best choice for our students. Later we will discuss how to construct your curriculum and how to evaluate its success.

The reasoning behind a skills-based curriculum went that knowledge will become obsolete in the future. Due to the internet and the accessibility of knowledge, freely available, to all mankind, students will not need to know facts and figures. Instead, they will need a range of flexible skills to allow them to tackle the jobs of the future. The argument goes that if a student can search for the information – for example, the process by which a bill becomes law – then they should only be judged on how they can apply those facts to a given scenario. They should be expected to show various thinking skills, like

---

2   Department for Education, *History Programmes of Study: Key Stage 3 – National Curriculum in England.* Ref: DFE-00194-2013 (2013). Available at: https://assets.publishing.service.gov.uk/government/uploads/system/uploads/attachment_data/file/239075/SECONDARY_national_curriculum_-_History.pdf.

3   D. P. Gardner et al., *A Nation at Risk: The Imperative for Education Reform* (Washington, DC: The National Commission on Excellence in Education, 1983). Available at: https://files.eric.ed.gov/fulltext/ED226006.pdf.

problem-solving and creativity, within this context. So, education should emphasise the demonstration of these traits over the acquisition of relevant knowledge.

Cognitively, this is a load of nonsense. Knowledge is the prerequisite for skills within any domain. Try teaching any skill – for example, making a cup of tea. There is a certain amount of knowledge required for the skill to be acquired successfully. Firstly, there are the *declarative facts,* those which can be seen as objective. In this case, these are all the objects involved, their locations and intrinsic properties. Then there is the *procedural knowledge*: the knowledge associated with how things fit together in a sequence. In this case, it would include the operation of the equipment (tap, kettle, etc.) as well as the sequence of techniques (how to use a tea bag, straining, the addition of milk, etc.). So, the skill of making a decent cup of tea is in fact the culmination of a large body of different types of knowledge, as Figure 1 shows.

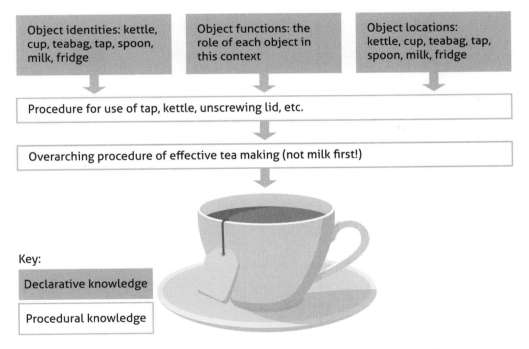

Figure 1: Making a cup of tea

Declarative knowledge: Knowledge about facts.

Procedural knowledge: Knowledge about how to do something.

This is often ignored by those favouring a skills-based, 21st-century curriculum because they suffer from the *curse of knowledge*, which impacts their ability to communicate effectively.[4] In a skills-based curriculum the danger is that the teacher takes the knowledge they have acquired for granted and assumes that everyone else has already acquired it. This is a potentially dangerous choice and often disadvantages those students who have missed certain assumed experiences.

> **Curse of knowledge:** A well-demonstrated cognitive bias, meaning that an individual falsely assumes that others have the same background information as they have.

In the example of making a cup of tea, the knowledge required might be too familiar and obvious, and you might remain unconvinced. So, to illustrate this further, consider learning to drive. In Figure 2 I've tried to break down driving in the same way.

Object identities: accelerator, brake, clutch, handbrake, wipers, lights and other dashboard controls, battery, fuel cap, fluids, etc.	Object functions: the role of each object in this context. In this case particularly the role of the accelerator, ignition, clutch and brake	Object locations: Right hand drive, common layouts of cars, exceptions for this particular car	The Highway Code

Procedure for starting the car, using the clutch and brakes

Manoeuvres (e.g. three-point turn, turn in road, parking, etc.)

Application of the Highway Code to different contexts

Figure 2: How to drive a car

4 J. Kennedy, Debiasing the Curse of Knowledge in Audit Judgment, *The Accounting Review*, 70(2) (1995): 249–273.

Driving is a complex process, so it is a great analogy for learning in any context. I've put the majority of the most basic requirements in the diagram but have ignored how knowledge of differing weather conditions impacts decisions for simplicity's sake. Notice how driving has a significant extra domain of knowledge: the Highway Code. I am sure that if you were asked to recall the rules of the Highway Code, you would be far from encyclopaedic, just like I am. However, you will know most of the basic rules of the road. You might not be able to fully recall this prior knowledge, but it will be demonstrated by the choices you make in the moment.[5] It's there in the background as *tacit knowledge*, helping you to perform a complex task with relative ease on a daily basis.

> **Tacit knowledge:** Knowledge that is gained through experience and is hard to communicate to others because we are unaware it exists.

Let's consider two anecdotes about learning to drive as illustrations of the power of knowledge. I learnt to drive when I was about 17 and a half. It took me 25 lessons and two practical tests. Like a typical teen, it took me ages to master the clutch, but also many lessons to learn the rules about junctions, the size of an adequate gap to pull out into, etc. My friend Bill did not learn to drive until he was in his early thirties. Like me, his first few lessons focused on the basic controls and in this respect he was equally poor. His instructor predicted that he would need at least 25 lessons. Within 12 lessons he had passed his test. Once he had grasped how to use the mechanical functions of the car, he was ready. He already had years of experience of the Highway Code as an attentive adult passenger. He was relatively fluent in how the rules were applied as he had witnessed a large array of situations in real life. He just had an inability to physically control the car. His prior knowledge accelerated his progress in the skill of driving.

A knowledge-rich curriculum is not devoid of skills; it prioritises the acquisition of knowledge before it is successfully applied using skills. This explains why teachers often complain about students' skills being non-transferrable. How often do teachers bemoan that a student's writing skills do not translate from English into other subjects? Or that they can form a coherent argument in history but not in literature; they can analyse a painting and its imagery but not a poem; they can evaluate evidence from a science experiment but not climate data in geography? This is evidence of the domain-specific nature of knowledge.

A student will first gain *inflexible* knowledge that is completely limited to the area in which it was originally taught. As their expertise improves, they will develop *flexible*

---

5   C. Nebel, Learning 'Useless' Things in School is (Usually) NOT Useless, *The Learning Scientists* [blog] (7 February 2020). Available at: https://www.learningscientists.org/blog/2020/2/7-1.

knowledge that can be applied more broadly and to a wider variety of situations. The ability to execute the widest application of the most flexible knowledge is often called 'creativity' or 'problem-solving skills'. When a student has flexible knowledge, they can bring knowledge across multiple domains and synthesise new ideas from existing rules and patterns. The journey to this stage is different for each person and each domain, based on a multitude of genetic and environmental factors. Creativity and problem-solving are the hardest to achieve, and often we are tempted to try and skip to the end by teaching them as explicit skills. This is not efficient, and we often end up with a shadow of the teacher's ideas parroted back by the student.

As an example, when I was in Year 11, I had to do a piece of chemistry coursework. At the time, coursework was aimed at providing a chance for students to work independently and demonstrate their planning and practical skills. The whole class was given the following brief: using common laboratory equipment, determine the rate of reaction for calcium carbonate in different concentrations of acid. My chemistry teacher made his instructions specific. He pointed out where all the equipment was and made it clear that how we proceeded was our own choice. The whole class set to work. Five minutes later I came up to the front with a long list of equipment that I wanted to use for an experiment based on the idea that carbon dioxide turns limewater cloudy, which would affect the amount of light that can pass through a sample. He read the list and then stood up. He beckoned me over to the corner of the lab and pointed to the class. 'Look at the rest of the class. I can get you all of this if you want but you could just do that.' He said it in a whisper. Everyone else was using a simple change in mass method using a timer and a balance. I quickly went back to my place and copied my friend's method. At the end of the lesson the teacher pulled me aside. 'That was an interesting idea; you'd be a good chemist if you tried harder.' That was the day I decided to study chemistry at A level.[6]

I have often thought about why I didn't think to use such an obvious solution. Perhaps I was away when that method was covered in class or I just was not concentrating? This story demonstrates two things: firstly, that you need prior knowledge to solve problems efficiently. Your potential solutions must be based on something that you already know. Secondly, I was able to devise my own solution due to my knowledge of chemistry being somewhat flexible, which my teacher recognised as advantageous for A-level study. So, from a cognitive perspective, knowledge-based curricula are not rote learning at the expense of creativity. They are in fact about providing the necessary foundation of knowledge to allow creativity to blossom.

---

6   I realise that this anecdote is actually an admission of malpractice on the teacher's part. I'm sure the statute of limitations has passed. Please don't take away my coordinated science GCSE!

The case for a knowledge-rich curriculum

Michael F. D. Young is a sociologist who has written extensively on the role curricula play in developing society. In his 2010 paper, Three Educational Scenarios for the Future, he and his collaborator Johan Muller set out possible future societies based on how they value knowledge within their respective education systems.[7] They look at how school knowledge is separated from non-school knowledge. By looking at each in turn we can gain a better understanding of the stakes in the knowledge vs skills debate.

Future 1: boundaries are given and fixed

This is a naturalised or under-socialised concept of knowledge. In this future, knowledge belongs to the elite – whether they be elite by birth or wealth. In this system only those who can engage in elite society are able to access knowledge. This was the pervasive system in most European cultures up until the end of the 19th century. As society developed and mass education was established, a two-tier system began to form. The elites received the best knowledge from the best teachers at the best facilities. To avoid the obvious inequality in the system becoming apparent to the rest of the populace, a small number of non-elites could enter the elite education system based on merit. This system is labelled a 'meritocracy', ignoring the fact that it is structured to maintain a divide between the two halves of society. Future 1 allows everyone to access education, but non-elites get a watered-down, vocationally focused curriculum that prevents them from truly accessing the social elite. Socially conservative Future 1 offers a world in which the education system is designed to reinforce the class divide. This is not *powerful knowledge* but *knowledge for the powerful*. The knowledge valued by the elites in Future 1 is traditional and remains stagnant.

While it might seem strange to regard this as a possible future, when it seems so fixated on the past, elements of Future 1 are enduring features of most education systems. The British grammar and independent school systems, for example. Teaching in Future 1 aims to be content obsessed, with an emphasis on rote learning. The aim is complete recall of all facts, no matter their importance, as this is how it has always been done. Tradition rules all.

---

7   M. Young and J. Muller, Three Educational Scenarios for the Future: Lessons from the Sociology of Knowledge, *European Journal of Education*, 45(1) (2010): 11–27. DOI: 10.1111/j.1465-3435.2009.01413.x.

Future 2: the end of boundaries

This future moves towards an 'over-socialised' concept of knowledge. Future 2 aims to deconstruct the barriers in education as a response to the existence of Future 1. As labour markets' existing boundaries blur, Future 2 focuses on a series of generalisable educational concepts. Digital technologies and student-directed work turn teachers from instructors into facilitators. Curricula shift to prevent the segregation found in Future 1 and become more skill-based and generic, with subjects becoming merged. Summative feedback is less useful when differentiating students against such broad criteria. Unfortunately, social boundaries are very real and the de-differentiation of the system does not remove them, it merely makes them invisible. This sends low-income students – the very ones Future 2 wants to help the most – down a path of low-value courses which limit their future academic potential. Future 2 was very much the agenda of the then Labour government's education policy at the turn of the millennium, with multiple academic and vocational pathways leading many students away from powerful knowledge. This, in turn, limits their potential access to certain areas of society.

Teaching in Future 2 rejects rote learning in favour of generalisations, with topics explored only at a superficial level. It is down to the teacher's specialist expertise to decide what important information is delivered to students. This creates inequality within the education system, disproportionately affecting schools in deprived areas, which struggle to recruit and retain expert teachers. Student-led pedagogy leads to students learning important content to varying depths at varying speeds. As time passes, it is harder to progress as no one knows what prior knowledge each student has from their previous years of study. The outcome of Future 2 is a lack of clarity within the labour market about students' capabilities and about which candidates are most qualified for a position. As students progress through the system, they become acutely aware of their gaps and are forced to play catch-up against their peers if they wish to proceed.

Future 3: boundaries are maintained but can be crossed by acquiring new knowledge

Future 3 recognises that boundaries between disciplinary bodies of knowledge exist. These boundaries are not dictated by societal structures but arise between subjects and areas of expertise. This is not to say that these disciplines are completely immovable; over time the boundaries will shift, and new disciplines might emerge. Subjects often begin to blur into each other at the highest level – for example, bioinformatics: a blend of biology, computer science and maths – but these interdisciplinary subjects still contain clearly defined disciplines within them. There is therefore a strong case for having clearly defined boundaries at a primary and secondary school level. Future 3 recognises historical barriers to education for lower-income students and aims to provide students with the knowledge required to cross these barriers; to convert the *knowledge of the powerful* into *powerful knowledge*. Any student from any background can access the knowledge and skills needed to excel within that specialist subject, regardless of their socio-economic status.

The main issue with Future 3 is with deciding what the best knowledge is – how do we know what students should know? Teachers might not always be best placed to decide. They often come from a variety of backgrounds and have differing levels of expertise. All subjects have world-leading expert communities and through looking at these experts' work and consulting them it is possible to create a list of 'best knowledge' in a subject. In fact, one of the benefits of Future 3 is that it allows expert communities to delicately balance knowledge and skills within their subject. For example, powerful knowledge in product design will contain knowledge about how various common machining techniques are used in a variety of scenarios, and the skill to apply this knowledge. Furthermore, Future 3 includes the disciplinary knowledge of how new knowledge is created within a subject. So, students become equipped with the powerful knowledge of how each discipline expands – for example, the role of experimentation in science. It is important to recognise that this does not mean that students are educated using the same methods as the discipline uses. The pedagogy used to teach should be chosen based on what is best for learning. For example, we should not force students to learn maths via investigation just because mathematical concepts were initially discovered this way.

> **Substantive knowledge:** Knowledge which is taught as fact.
>
> **Disciplinary knowledge:** Knowledge of how a given subject or domain expands its agreed knowledge.

My own personal belief is that now more than ever we are able to create Future 3. By allowing teachers to deliver a powerful knowledge curriculum as they see fit, we can give students from less-privileged backgrounds the knowledge to access society at whatever level they choose. Future 3's honesty about the societal nature of powerful knowledge is empowering, and its use of disciplinary knowledge as well as substantive knowledge illustrates to students that each subject expands their knowledge in different ways.

Your curriculum ethos

I hope that I have managed to convince you of the value of a knowledge-rich curriculum. If not, then that does not mean the rest of this chapter will be useless to you; it just means we each have a different ethos. Your ethos will inform all the decisions you make. While I am not a huge fan of having a mission statement plastered all over the walls and on every letterhead, I do think that being able to refer back to your ethos is incredibly useful. Curriculum planning is a marathon, not a sprint. You need to accept that it might take years. The first draft might need to be ready for September, but it will, and should, evolve over time. Your ethos, however, should be your one commandment, so to speak, etched on stone and a constant in your thinking.

The range and scope of your curriculum

Should you create a vastly expanded curriculum that explores all areas of the subject you lead? Should you choose to focus on the most vital areas at the expense of some of the fringe areas? How do you know which topics are more important than others? Too much choice can be paralysing, especially under time constraints. Ignoring any legal requirements, from a purely pragmatic point of view, we will use the national curriculum as our starting point.

The model of curriculum you choose will be highly dependent on the subject you teach. Ruth Ashbee has been working hard to create a common language to describe the differences in the way knowledge is structured and acquired in different subjects.[8] Some subject knowledge is highly *hierarchical* in nature. Hierarchical subjects have certain knowledge that must be gained by students if they are to carry on learning. Maths is a classically hierarchical subject. Conversely, art is not particularly hierarchical; its structure is *horizontal*. You could look at art through the lenses of multiple techniques – for example, sculpture or painting. While you might have strong feelings about which aspects of art need to be taught first, you'll probably encounter equally valid but opposing ideas. In the case of maths, new knowledge must be *integrated* into the existing knowledge domain. The aim of maths as a discipline is to find truths that are generalisable to multiple contexts and in agreement with existing mathematical laws. In the case of art, knowledge expands in an *accumulative* manner. Artists either expand on existing fields

8   R. Ashbee, Vertical, Horizontal, Hierarchical, Cumulative, Integrative, Discursive, *The Fruits Are Sweet* [blog] (11 February 2020). Available at: https://rosalindwalker.wordpress.com/2020/02/11/vertical-horizontal-hierarchical-cumulative-integrative-discursive/.

– say, impressionism – or develop a completely new approach. They do not have to be compliant with the objective rules of the domain to be classed as art.

What does this mean for us as curriculum leaders? Well, it tells us a lot about the freedom we have in sequencing our subject. In our maths example, we probably have very little freedom regarding what is taught in each year or key stage; we will mostly be building on concepts that have come before. Whereas in art we could decide that each year will have a different focus – for example, drawing or sculpture – or we could explore many mediums within a more holistic topic – for example, African art.

Figures 3 and 4 are stylised visual representations of a horizontal curriculum and a hierarchical curriculum. The shapes represent key knowledge, skills and concepts that must be learnt; the lines indicate how these could relate to one another.

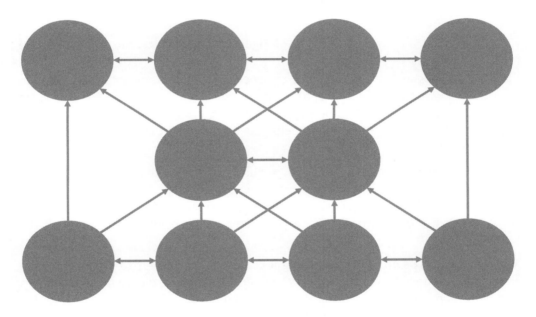

Figure 3: A horizontal curriculum structure

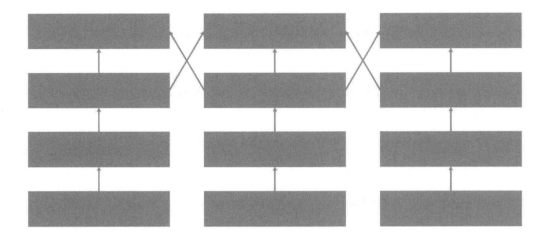

Figure 4: A hierarchical curriculum structure

Notice how in Figure 3 there are plenty of opportunities for interrelationships between concepts – shown by the diagonal and double-headed arrows. As a leader, you could plan a route through these in a multitude of ways. Granted, this is an oversimplification; I am sure that there are some routes that would be much more efficient than others, but the possibilities are there.

In contrast, in Figure 4 there are few opportunities to explore interrelationships because we are looking at a hierarchy. The options do improve as you journey through the curriculum, but students require a large amount of specialist knowledge in order to make the leaps between the subdomains. These structures will also inform the depth of the curriculum.

When discussing depth of understanding it is common for leaders to instantly assume that more is better. 'We teach our Year 7s *The Crucible* because we have high standards and deliver an ambitious curriculum,' an English curriculum leader might proclaim. But can Year 7 students engage with the themes of McCarthyism and persecution that make *The Crucible* an important piece of literature? Or will they only be able to engage with it at a superficial level? Is there an opportunity cost to your students? What if it was taught in Year 9 after students have studied the Cold War briefly in history during Year 8?

> **Opportunity cost:** The cost that is incurred because you can only do one thing at a time. Time spent on one activity is time that cannot be spent performing another task.

Conversely, teaching Year 7 about subatomic particles is a good example of an ambitious curriculum. Yes, it is part of the GCSE science specification, but there is no objective reason why they cannot learn it early. The knowledge is not conceptually harder than the names of the organs; it is just slightly more abstract due to its size. More importantly, knowledge of protons and electrons allows students to gain a deeper understanding of physics and chemistry as they progress into Years 8 and 9.

An ambitious, knowledge-rich curriculum needs to prioritise what content is to be taught and specify to what depth students are expected to master it if it is to be effective. This might seem a bit theoretical for a book which is intended to be practical in application, but understanding how your subject is structured allows you to explicitly create a sequence that works for your context.

Sequencing your curriculum

What is the best way to tell the story of your subject? What things are so crucial that all students deserve to know them?

When building your curriculum, you will probably start with a broad outline of the content you want the students to learn. If you are following the national curriculum, it will break down certain concepts that must be learnt in a particular year or key stage. After that, the rest is up to you. This freedom can be daunting and often results in leaders just sequencing the curriculum in the way in which they were taught it or the way in which it has always been sequenced in their school. This might well be the best solution, but we owe it to our students to interrogate our curriculum to ensure that we have explored all the options and have a solid rationale.

At the same time, we must be pragmatic. We teach in real schools with real issues, like staffing, timetabling, and the number of lessons students have in our subject each week. We have to make balanced choices and prioritise what is best for the students but accept that practicalities might mean compromise. We are going to look at the sequencing of the curriculum at three levels:

1 Between years.

2 Within a year.

3 Within an individual topic.

For simplicity, I use the word 'topic', but I recognise in some subjects – for example, English – other words might be more appropriate.

Between years

When should you teach graphing in maths? Should your history topics be taught chronologically at Key Stage 3? These decisions cannot be made in isolation. Subjects with overriding links – for example, science and maths – need to be carefully sequenced with consideration for each other. If the maths department teaches graphing skills in Year 8, but the science department expects students to be able to plot graphs in Year 7, then a lot of time will be used teaching students how to plot graphs in those science lessons – material which might then be retrodden in Year 8 maths.

We also need to consider progression through the years, both in terms of content and context. Some topics require prior knowledge to ensure that students can access them. Do the topics in Year 8 naturally build and expand on those taught in Year 7? Crucially, does the context become more ambitious? Does it provide the necessary exemplification of the new knowledge and skills for this year? Is it more nuanced than the previous year? All these factors play a role in the decision-making process, which is why building a curriculum takes time and a lot of thought.

Within a year

Once the topics for each year are agreed, and their fit with related subjects has been checked, then we can consider the individual topic within a year. In a perfect world we would just decide which topics are linked by content and skills and introduce them in the most appropriate order. Unfortunately, we might not have the lesson time needed to enact our vision, and we might have to split a class between multiple teachers. On top of that, we might not have access to specialist equipment as often as we would like. Running a large science department, I faced all of these issues. We had to split classes due to timetabling constraints. We had a limited amount of equipment for certain practicals and a small percentage of classes were not taught in a specialist science lab. This resulted in us having to teach topics in parallel and in rotation. That way students had one consistent teacher delivering a cohesive topic of concepts, even if they had to learn two subjects during the fortnightly timetable cycle.

By teaching topics in rotation, we ensured that all students could do practical work in the right sequence – they didn't have to miss out, or do things in an unhelpful order, because the equipment was being used by another class. The downside was that every scheme of work needed to ensure that it did not assume prior knowledge from topics taught in that rotation. For example, if you had planned to teach density in physics, you would need to plan in the explanation of particle arrangements so that any students who had not been taught this would be able to access the concept. This is not necessarily a bad thing, as we will discuss in Chapter 2. Reviewing prior knowledge is a vital part of all lessons. Again, we come back to the concept of opportunity cost: time spent doing one thing means we can't do something else.

Within a topic

Writing a successful scheme of work for a topic is highly dependent on the teacher's expertise. Subject experts instinctively know the overall narrative arc that the topic should follow. They also know the twists in the tale, the nooks and crannies that students tend to get lost in, and the background stories to enhance students' understanding of the concepts and their cultural relevance. But what if you are not a subject specialist? What if you are new to leading the curriculum? Below is a summary of Ruth Ashbee's attempt to try to make processes of knowledge organisation explicit:[9]

- **Concrete before abstract.** This seems obvious at first glance but often it is overlooked. Learners find concepts easier to understand if they have knowledge of concrete representations of the concept before learning its abstract definition. When planning our topics, we need to ensure that all the necessary concrete concepts are in place before introducing the abstract. Pritesh Raichura, head of science at Michaela Community School, gives a great example about homeostasis.[10] Instead of beginning the lesson with the definition of the concept, he first builds on the students' concrete experiences of how their bodies change when exercising. This provides a foundation of concrete understanding before introducing the more abstract definition of the term. This is really important when dealing with abstract mathematical ideas like direct or inverse proportionality. In the humanities, teaching a concept like migration could begin by exploring a specific case – for example, a personal story or an historical event – then defining migrations and establishing reasons and consequences.

- **Simple to complex.** Our scheme of work needs to build from the simplest concepts to the more complex, and our examples and non-examples – those things that exemplify what a concept is not, in order to illustrate its boundaries – should also build from simple to complex. Sometimes experts choose poor examples and

9 R. Ashbee, The 10 Features of Highly Effective Curriculum Planning, *Reflections in Science Education* [blog] (11 February 2019). Available at: https://reflectionsinscience.wordpress.com/2019/02/11/the-10-features-of-highly-effective-curriculum-planning-a-guest-blog/.

10 P. Raichura, Clear Teacher Explanations 1: Examples and Non-Examples, *Bunsen Blue* [blog] (20 October 2019). Available at: https://bunsenblue.wordpress.com/2019/10/20/clear-teacher-explanations-i-examples-non-examples/.

ignore key exceptions or complexities because they make sense according to their advanced knowledge schema, or they think that the examples are more exciting and engaging. This leads to students not understanding where and when a particular piece of knowledge, or a particular skill, needs to be applied.

- **Constituents to the whole.** It is important that we make sure that our curriculum is planned so that students encounter relevant prior knowledge, and have the opportunity to practise it to a level of confidence, before a new concept is introduced. Sometimes this will require checking back through previous years' work to make sure that the required numeracy and other skills have been well covered. If students have not had the time and opportunity to become capable in the component aspects, they will struggle when we introduce the concept that uses them all in connection. At best, they will learn the new skill as isolated, inflexible knowledge. We also need to consider how we build meaning and narrative across the years. What prior experiences and concepts do students need in order to appreciate the curriculum's narrative? What themes will we weave throughout? Are there certain elements of cultural capital that need to be introduced earlier so that all students can engage with the current topic (and are we assuming that students will be familiar with these)? How does our current work link to other subjects, prior work, or potential careers? Online subject communities are excellent places to find discussion, debate and research on these questions and possible solutions. Students need enough time to work on the different components and master them, and lessons should be structured with consideration to retrieval practice to ensure that key ideas can be brought to mind when needed. This will be discussed in more detail in Chapter 2.

How can we evaluate the curriculum?

Leading the curriculum is, frankly, a daunting task, and we haven't yet considered how our decisions affect our teaching and learning policy (Chapter 2) or our assessment policy (Chapter 3). In reality, all these areas will constantly interact, but it is vital that they all conform to our ethos: our one commandment. Otherwise, we are at risk of assessment leading teaching and curriculum decisions.

Evaluation of the curriculum is a cyclical process that starts with our ethos. In my department, our shared ethos is to deliver 'Powerful knowledge that allows students of all backgrounds to have limitless futures.' Yes, it is a bit buzzwordy, but beneath that lies a valid core intention: to ensure that all students, no matter their background, have access to the best of what has been thought and said so that they can pursue any career of their choice. This ethos is the lens through which we evaluate our curriculum design. We start, therefore, with the content and ask the following questions:

- Are we teaching anything that is not powerful knowledge?

- Are we missing anything that we would deem to be powerful knowledge?

We can look at the example of teaching rocks as a topic in science. This is traditionally a Year 8 topic and it is in the national curriculum. Academies, however, do not have to follow the national curriculum. There is no earth science in the GCSE anymore, so academies can say, 'Why should we teach it? Why don't we cut it out then? After all, schools are there to help kids get grades, aren't they?' I politely disagree. A school that has outcomes as its only objective probably paraphrased their ethos from the early 21st-century American street philosopher Curtis James Jackson III (aka 50 Cent): get grades or die tryin'.

In fact, despite its removal from the GCSE specification, understanding rock formation, volcanic and earthquake activity and the Earth's cycles (water, weather, etc.) enables students to engage more confidently in current debates around climate change and equips them with a better understanding of the environment on a global scale. We feel that it is important to teach students about rocks. However, we should also consider the potential overlap with geography. There are aspects of this topic that we might be able to remove from the science curriculum without the students being disadvantaged.

Finding the evidence

Schools are awash with data. Chapter 4 will look at the pros and cons of commonly used data and how it impacts decisions. You might want to look at data and at question level analysis to understand where in the curriculum students are performing well and where they are struggling. However, as we will discuss in detail in Chapter 3, assuming that students perform poorly on a particular task *because* the curriculum is poorly constructed is fraught with danger. A much better approach is to get teachers to reflect on students' performance and to note any common areas that they found difficult. These can then be discussed and categorised as curriculum issues, teaching issues or non-issues.

Snag lists

The end of the year is a terrible time to try to evaluate the entire curriculum. It will be nearly impossible to remember all of the small issues that cropped up along the way. The best time to take action is when the issues arise: unfortunately, that is also when you lack free time. My solution is to have a snag list. This is quite simply a list of things that need further thought or fixing. It might be big issues about sequencing, or small things like the need to include a certain example or non-example in a particular lesson. We can also record our thoughts on how to improve next year's curriculum – for example, by making links between topics or subjects or exploring more external opportunities for our students. By having a document that is live and readily available, staff can actively contribute by noting their issues. This gives you much better coverage of the entire curriculum – as you are unlikely to teach all of it yourself – and it empowers all staff to have an input. This helps to ensure that the curriculum is a living, breathing thing at the heart of your department and that everyone is aware of the ethos, implementation and enactment of the curriculum in your context.

Figure 5 offers an example of a simple layout for a snag list, which allows you to note where and when the issues arise and their priority. You can scan it quickly and possibly resolve small issues or schedule time to deal with high-priority problems. Fixes are small improvements to existing pathways or resources. Additions ask staff to add new ideas, analogies, examples or strategies which the entire department would find useful. These could come from the staff directly or from books and blogs on the topic.

Year	Topic code	Brief note of issue	Fix or addition	Priority (low/medium/high)

Figure 5: A simple snag list

Recap

- Curriculum is the most important area that you can be asked to lead on. It is much more than merely sequencing topics; it is how you share your ethos and educational values beyond your own classroom.

- A knowledge-rich curriculum offers the best hope of a socially mobile future for students of all backgrounds. All students have the right to powerful knowledge.

- When designing your curriculum, you need to start with sequencing and ensure that you work from concrete to abstract, from simple to complex, and from the constituents to the whole.

- Try to think of the curriculum on three levels: between years, within a year, and within a topic.

- There will always be pragmatic trade-offs that will have to be made, but try to let your ethos guide you as far as you can.

- When evaluating your curriculum, do not leave it until the summer. Keep track of issues throughout the year with your team. Prioritise and find time to fix critical issues as they arise.

- Do not let data be the tail that wags the dog. Question level analysis does not tell you as much about the success of the curriculum as you might think.

- Actively engage with subject communities and other teachers. Twitter is a great way to discover educational researchers, subject community leaders and fellow teachers. Each subject has an association which might also provide valuable insights. If you're not a fan of social media, you might want to find a school in a similar context that is further along in their curriculum journey and plan a visit.

Reflect

- Where do I stand in the knowledge vs skills debate?

- What is my personal ethos for our curriculum?

- What type of curriculum will serve the needs of my students?

- Is my curriculum well sequenced? Does it tell a cohesive story of my subject?

- What evidence is there to support my decisions? Do I have to use data or will other qualitative measures give me insight into the effectiveness of the curriculum?

- What does my subject community have to say on what makes a strong curriculum? Do I have all the information I need?

- Can I justify the compromises I might have to make to ensure that my subject fits within the school's wider vision?

Chapter 2

Leading teaching and learning

Memory is the residue of thought.

Daniel Willingham[1]

Leading the development of teaching and learning is a lynchpin of middle leadership. When all is said and done, middle leaders have a large array of responsibilities but ensuring that the best possible teaching is happening in all lessons, so all students are learning, is the most important role.

The area of teaching and learning is large and diverse. There are many books, blogs and talks devoted to it, so the chance of me covering all the aspects involved here are slim. In this chapter I want to discuss why the link between teaching and learning is less obvious than is often assumed, summarise some of the best ideas available on effective teaching, and discuss how to communicate them to a team. I opened this chapter with what I consider to be the most important sentence in education, from cognitive scientist Daniel Willingham. It's worth reading again right now.

Let me be clear: that idea changed my teaching. It is ludicrous to think that I hadn't explicitly realised this sooner: I mean, it is obvious, isn't it? Throughout my teacher training and early career I had never really considered memory to be important. I was trained to understand that for students to learn the most they needed to experience everything through their preferred learning style. I was told that if I could capture their imagination with awe and wonder then they would absorb the relevant information and become knowledgeable. I take solace in the fact that I was not the only one. The bad lessons hashtag (#badlessons) on Twitter has seen myriad teachers sharing their misguided lesson ideas from years ago.

I hope you were not as clueless as I was as a trainee. Before we go into the details about what learning might be and how it might happen, let us quickly look at one of my terrible

---

1   D. T. Willingham, *Why Don't Students Like School? A Cognitive Scientist Answers Questions About How the Mind Works and What It Means for the Classroom* (San Francisco, CA: Jossey-Bass, 2009), p. 41.

ideas as an example not to follow. Later I will illustrate exactly why I now realise it is a bad idea – of course, this may be obvious to you as you read on.

The 'expert visit'

I was teaching a Year 9 class the old variation topic. We had just covered cloning and genetic engineering. I wanted to do a hot-seat activity in which the students plan questions to ask an expert. I told them that I knew an expert geneticist who had studied genetics at university and was coming in next week to answer their questions. I asked them to write their questions about the future of genetic engineering in the back of their books and also set this as a homework task.

The lesson arrived and the students were really excited. 'Have we got a visitor today, sir?' was the greeting I received at the door from almost everyone. I got the students to sit in the front three rows and reminded them about the importance of showing good manners to guests. The door was in the far-left corner and my lab had a large, old-fashioned teacher bench at the front. I remember calling out, 'Oh, here he is!' As all the students turned to look at the door, they saw that it was shut and, through the window, they couldn't even see anyone waiting outside. When they turned back, they were presented with me and a shoebox. On the outside of the shoebox, the words 'DNA lab' were written in felt-tip pen. As their brows furrowed in confusion, out of the box popped a panda hand puppet!

What followed was my best Sooty and Sweep impression, with the panda (who I had named but can't remember what) whispering in my ear the answers to the students' questions. When they complained, I reminded them that the puppet was not really giving the answers and that I was in fact an expert on genetics, and had studied this at university. I had a great time and thought that the uniqueness of the event would help the students to recall the various pros and cons of genetic engineering.

What is learning?

Google tells me that learning is 'the acquisition of knowledge or skills through study, experience, or being taught'.[2] This definition seems to conveniently skip over that trickier aspect of the word: how do we know if something is learnt? If we consider a simple example – say, learning your phone number – we can elucidate some aspects of what learning means. If I were to ask you what your phone number is, I would expect you to be able to recall the number with ease. Your recital of the number is a demonstration of your ability to *perform* the task on demand. If you can perform a task on demand, can we say that you have learnt something? Well, maybe, but what if I had let you look at a piece of paper with your phone number written on it for 30 seconds and then asked the question? Suddenly the context has changed my belief that you really know the information and have not simply retained it in your brain for a short period of time. Clearly, a better demonstration of learning would be to wait for a period of time and then ask you to recite the phone number. Therefore, an improved definition of learning could be 'The ability to perform a skill or recall knowledge when required.'

It is true that not all learning is as easy to recall as a phone number. This is due to the nature of knowledge. In Chapter 1 we discussed declarative vs procedural knowledge. These categories were useful in allowing us to understand how we structure the curricular content. It is not just important to possess the knowledge required to perform the task but to know when the knowledge should be applied.

In his book *Applying Cognitive Science to Education*, physicist Fredrick Reif identifies two types of applicability conditions that an individual needs to be aware of if they are to correctly apply their knowledge:[3]

1   Validity conditions: the conditions in which use of the knowledge is valid. *Is it relevant to this question?*

2   Utility conditions: the potential outcomes of the knowledge. *Will it solve the problem we face?*

In the case of simple, declarative knowledge that exists in isolation – like a phone number – this is really easy to see in action. The validity and utility conditions are easy to define and essentially revolve around the question 'What is your phone number?' or 'How do I contact you?'

....

2   See https://www.lexico.com/definition/learning.
3   F. Reif, *Applying Cognitive Science to Education: Thinking and Learning in Scientific and Other Complex Domains* (Cambridge, MA: The MIT Press, 2008), pp. 37–38.

However, for other pieces of information these conditions are much less obvious. Consider the assassination of Archduke Franz Ferdinand. It is relatively easy to learn the declarative facts and procedural information related to this event. The hard part is understanding how and when to use the information, its limitations and the associated consequences. A student could have a strong grasp of the facts involved; they can retrieve them when asked, even after some time has passed, so we could say that they have learnt the facts. However, if they do not also learn the applicability conditions then they will not be able to correctly apply these facts – for example, when writing essays in history. This is another way of defining the flexibility of knowledge; if a student does not know or understand the applicability conditions, they will not be able to use their knowledge in contexts beyond simple recall. When we consider the implications of this for teaching and learning, we can see the value of explicitly illustrating the applicability conditions when explaining the material to students.

Following this reasoning, it seems that we might have to accept a simple but unnerving truth: learning might not happen in the classroom. When students complete a quiz at the end of the lesson, it doesn't mean that they have learnt the content – even if they score highly. It means that they comprehend what you explained to them and can perform the task that they have been set. For them to learn, they need to forget the work and revisit it subsequently. So, most likely, we can say that learning happens over time and possibly outside of the classroom. That the students can perform the task at the end of the lesson is by no means inconsequential; unfortunately, it just does not guarantee that they will learn the information better than a student who could not perform the task in the first instance.

If 'memory is the residue of thought', we need to understand how the brain works in more detail so that we can try to create optimal conditions to change our students' long-term memories. A common mistake is thinking that we think differently now than we did thousands of years ago. Because we have become much more civilised and effective as a society during the last few centuries – the thinking goes – our brains must have evolved too. Unfortunately, there is no evidence to suggest that this is the case. In fact, evidence suggests that modern Homo sapiens' brains probably developed about 35,000 years ago.[4]

4   B. Hays, First Came Homo Sapiens, Then Came the Modern Brain, *United Press International* (25 January 2018). Available at: https://www.upi.com/Science_News/2018/01/25/First-came-Homo-sapiens-then-came-the-modern-brain/6111516907001/.

The model of working memory

Cognitive scientists investigate how the mind works. They test theoretical models using experiments and measurements of brain activity because it's not yet possible to 'see' learning happen or a memory form directly. This book is not about comparing Atkinson and Shiffrin's 1968 multistore model[5] to other conceptualisations, such as Baddeley and Hitch's 1974 model of memory.[6] I do, however, want to introduce what Daniel Willingham calls a 'stripped-down model of the cognitive system', because it provides a very useful tool for analysing our decisions regarding teaching activities.[7]

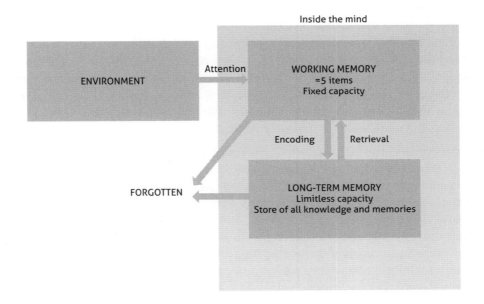

Figure 6: stripped-down model of the cognitive system

This model essentially breaks memory down to two areas: working memory (sometimes referred to as short-term memory) and long-term memory. Working memory is quite

5   R. C. Atkinson and R. M. Shiffrin, Human Memory: A Proposed System and Its Control Processes. In K. W. Spence and J. T. Spence (eds), *The Psychology of Learning and Motivation, Volume 2* (New York: Academic Press, 1968), pp. 89–195.

6   A. D. Baddeley and G. J. Hitch, Working Memory. In G. A. Bower (ed.), *Recent Advances in Learning and Motivation, Volume 8* (New York: Academic Press, 1974), pp. 47–89.

7   Adapted from D. T. Willingham, On Metaphor, Memory, and John King, *Daniel Willingham – Science & Education* [blog] (18 April 2016). Available at: http://www.danielwillingham.com/daniel-willingham-science-and-education-blog/on-metaphor-memory-and-john-king.

unimpressive at first glance. It has a very limited capacity – it appears to have a fixed range of five to nine items, which cannot be improved through training.[8] We can essentially see working memory as those things that you can keep active in your mind at the same time. As much as working memory is a disappointment, long-term memory is exceptional. It has unlimited storage for unknown durations of time. It is where we store declarative and procedural information, from the mundane – like where in the kitchen you go to find the ketchup – to the magnificent – like the life cycle of a star. The long-term memory also contains an archive of all our experiences and their relative connectivity.

We organise items in our long-term memory as schemas, which are networks of connected information. For example, if I asked you to consider the colour blue, you might instantly bring to mind various things that you associate with it. Some will be personal to you – say, the wallpaper in your bedroom – others will be more generalisable; you might think of the sky, or of shared cultural experiences – the TARDIS, for example. Your incredible brain will make these associations on its own, depending on the amount of time you have spent thinking about those things, or how often you've experienced them. Memory is the residue of thought, after all. We *encode* information from working memory into long-term memory and then *retrieve* it at a later date. The relative strength of this is down to practice. The more we try to retrieve a particular item, the easier it gets to do it.

I find this model particularly powerful for teachers due to its appreciation of the environment. In this model, the environment is everything outside of the mind. This includes – but is not limited to – the birds singing in the trees outside, that itch behind your ear, what the person sitting across the room is doing and, of course, for a student, their teacher. Only the things that catch students' attention will go into their working memory and only those that they pay close attention to will be effectively encoded into long-term memory. When you consider the limited capacity of working memory, it is a miracle we ever learn anything! Luckily for us we are very good at not paying attention to things. We generally forget about background noise and learn to focus on our teacher, for example.

If a student fills their working memory with task-irrelevant material, then the task-relevant information will not be processed and the student will not be able to encode this information into their long-term memory. The working memory model explains why students learn better when they are able to concentrate and have fewer distractions. It also explains why some students will swear blind that they have never been taught this before (when you know for a fact that they have): they simply were not paying attention at the time.

....

8 G. A. Miller, The Magical Number Seven, Plus or Minus Two: Some Limits on Our Capacity for Processing Information, *Psychological Review*, 63(2) (1956): 81–97.

This model has far-reaching implications for teachers. It forms a central part of John Sweller's cognitive load theory, which aims to explain the most effective ways to present new information without overloading working memory.[9] Table 1 tries to pull together the teaching and learning techniques from cognitive science which have a strong evidence base. Learning is a very murky subject and there are thousands of variables which are hard to control, but these approaches offer us the best options we have. I am sure that you will be familiar with some of them already, either from your own experimentation or from observing colleagues. I think that this list is our best bet at creating efficient and effective learning environments.

Table 1: Lessons from cognitive science and their implications for teachers

Aspect of cognitive science	Description	Implications for teachers
Expertise reversal effect	Experts learn better from problem-solving while novices learn better from explicit teacher instruction.	When introducing new material, it is best to explicitly explain it to students and only move onto problem-solving once they are proficient.
Testing effect	Students who were given practice tests performed better in the final exam than those who just reviewed their notes.	Testing is a learning experience, not just an assessment tool. Regular low-stakes testing (retrieval practice) aids performance.
Redundancy effect	Occurs when excess information affects learning. This could be because the information is irrelevant and so distracts from what needs to be learnt or because the information is doubled up in	Try not to read written text out loud to capable readers. Try to ensure the content of your resources is restricted to only relevant information.

9 J. Sweller, Cognitive Load Theory. In J. P. Mestre and B. H. Ross (eds), *The Psychology of Learning and Motivation: Volume 55. The Psychology of Learning and Motivation: Cognition in Education* (Cambridge, MA: Elsevier Academic Press, 2011), pp. 37–76.

Aspect of cognitive science	Description	Implications for teachers
Redundancy effect (cont.)	different forms. For example, the brain uses different channels to process visual and auditory information. Reading uses the auditory as well as the visual channels, so hearing and reading words simultaneously can overload working memory.	
Modality effect	Because the brain uses different channels for visual images and spoken words, displaying images and talking about them reduces interference and cognitive load.	Try to use relevant images and diagrams to structure your explanations. This can sometimes be called 'dual coding'.
Worked example effect	Providing worked examples helps reduce cognitive load and supports knowledge construction.	Providing worked examples allows students to see the desired outcome and provides a scaffold to help them complete work, especially if that work is new to them.
Completion problem effect	An extension of the worked example effect, this involves providing a partially complete example for students to finish.	Partially completed examples provide a level of scaffolding that reduces cognitive load and builds proficiency. Used together with worked examples, this is an example of the guidance fading effect.

Aspect of cognitive science	Description	Implications for teachers
Guidance fading effect	Students perform better when they complete a series of examples with increasing independence.	Students need to carefully move from fully worked examples to independent practice. Providing a series of examples with increasing amounts of missing information allows students to build fluency.
Variability effect	Providing problems with the same deep structure but different surface features, helps students to identify the deep structure of problems.	Varying examples to cover the range and scope of real-world examples demonstrates the applicability conditions of the knowledge.
Goal-free effect	Goal-free problems are those which do not specifically state the desired outcome. Instead, they invite students to find as many answers as possible. This increases the links between concepts and aids learning.	In certain situations (for example, when using diagrams, graphs and tables of data), goal-free problems can significantly enhance the learning of experienced students. However, this is not valuable for novices.
Activate prior knowledge	Novices learn better when new information is incorporated into a pre-existing schema.	Structure explanations so that they start by recapping prior learning or experience.
Deliver new information in chunks	New information is easier to understand if broken down into smaller units, then integrated (remember, simple to complex).	Plan explanations so that information is delivered in small, sequential chunks. Provide faded examples and slowly remove scaffolding as students gain expertise.

Aspect of cognitive science	Description	Implications for teachers
Spaced practice	Learning is more effective if carried out in small chunks spread over many days than condensed into a day.	Regular review of prior knowledge helps improve the chances of learning taking place.
Interleaving	Switching between related ideas improves students' ability to make links between ideas.	Make explicit links between relevant ideas and ask questions which get them thinking about both topics.
Stories are powerful learning tools	People remember information told in story form much more easily than isolated facts. This is because stories have emotional resonance and narrative structures that help organise the information.	Relevant, concise stories are very powerful learning tools. Stories work best when they have the four Cs:[10] 1 Causality: events must matter and have consequences. 2 Conflict: there must be an opposition to provide a challenge. 3 Complications: there must not be an easy path to tread. 4 Characters: there must be ways of identifying the different players in the story and their qualities. The actions of great characters are the best way to tell a story.

10 D. T. Willingham, Ask the Cognitive Scientist: The Privileged Status of Story, The American Educator (summer 2004). Available at: https://www.aft.org/periodical/american-educator/summer-2004/ask-cognitive-scientist.

Aspect of cognitive science	Description	Implications for teachers
Avoid seductive details	Seductive details are those which capture the imagination but distract from the important message of the explanation.	Make sure that any anecdotal diversions in explanations clearly illustrate the key ideas. Choosing interesting but less-relevant contexts can reduce learning.

One of the problems for the theory of working memory is the issue of performing complex tasks – for example, reading. If working memory is limited to roughly seven items, how can we read fluently and with speed? When we are young, we learn to read by building up words from their constituent phonemes; when we are older, that appears to happen almost instantly. How can we do that if we can only hold seven phonemes in our working memory? How can we read words with more than seven phonemes, like *incomprehensible*?

Luckily for us, the brain can 'chunk' simple, frequently used items into a schema that can be processed as one item. So, to a competent reader, the word 'incomprehensible' could be a schema and forms just one item. Familiar phrases can even be condensed into a single schema. Complex schemas with strong internal associations can be accessed quickly and automatically. Consider the famous Knowledge – the test that London black cab drivers must pass. According to this model, those who have studied and mastered the entire map of the streets of London have secured large areas of it as one strongly connected schema, allowing them to devote more resources to accounting for the time of day, traffic patterns and their equally famous small talk![11] For those of us who have not learnt the Knowledge, a single unfamiliar route across London will be a series of procedural steps that we would have to remember, were it not for written directions or a handy satnav.

One thing that helps to create these condensed units, or schemas, is practice. When we practise a musical instrument – or, as we explored in Chapter 1, learn to drive – we begin with a series of independent actions which each need their own space in working memory. By practising these skills, we gain fluency and a degree of automaticity. With considerable practice, we can perform the skills automatically and without large amounts of conscious thought. This explains why drivers can focus on the road and the route they are taking instead of putting all of their focus into clutch control.

....

11 Reif, *Applying Cognitive Science to Education*, pp. 32–36.

As teachers, we need to provide enough time and support for our students to practise the given task. Even more learning can arise if we plan the task to make the students think about a concept from multiple angles. We will essentially be soliciting the same answers but in various different ways. We can also take advantage of interleaving and spaced practice by revising content during relevant activities later in the year. For example, if we want students to know that the cell contains a nucleus which holds the genetic information of the organism, we can start by asking, 'What is the role of the nucleus?' 'Where is the nucleus found?' Later we can rearrange these questions to make students think about the same facts but asking something different. We might say, 'What holds genetic material in an animal cell?' Then later we might ask students to correct the mistakes in this sentence: *Plant cells have all their genetic material stored in their chloroplasts.* There are many more ways to generate the answers we want. Each new way increases the encoding of this fact into the long-term memory. By asking some questions during the initial teaching and then others at a later date – for example, during a lesson about related content – we can further enhance the encoding of the fact into long-term memory.

With this understanding we can adapt our definition of learning even further. We can now say that 'learning is a change in long-term memory',[12] with an understanding of the reasoning behind this and the appreciation for its significance in our teaching practice. With our understanding of what cognitive science says about the learning process and our new definition of learning, we can begin to build some core principles for teaching and learning.

Looking back at my example of misguided practice when my 'expert visitor' came to visit, we can understand why it was such a bad idea. Firstly, the students did not know enough to write decent questions; it takes a large amount of knowledge to identify the gaps and synthesise a question which will fill them. I hadn't devoted any lesson time to practising or embedding the concepts; I had just taught each lesson and moved on because they got the bingo questions right in the plenary. The students had a superficial understanding and thus couldn't come up with anything meaningful to ask. At the time I solved this problem by circulating around the classroom at pace, drip-feeding questions into students' work through discussion and then calling on them in front of the class and praising them for their work (which was actually mine).

Secondly, some of the students were really annoyed that I had tricked them. They just sulked in the corner. Strong emotional responses can be a real hindrance. They deliberately withheld their attention as an act of retribution. Thirdly, most just remembered the panda and not the actual discussion. If memory is the residue of thought, then those

12 P. A. Kirschner, J. Sweller and R. E. Clark, Why Minimal Guidance During Instruction Does Not Work: An Analysis of the Failure of Constructivist, Discovery, Problem-Based, Experiential, and Inquiry-Based Teaching, *Educational Psychologist*, 41(2) (2006): 75–86 at 75.

students learnt that I owned a panda hand puppet and that I was a liar. To make matters worse, the discussion had no structured follow-up to consolidate the students' ideas and emphasise key concepts. After all, the discussion was supposed to be so engaging that all the knowledge would be instantly absorbed! Hot-seat activities often fall down because offering the amount of support that the students need in order to craft their questions takes longer than just embedding the key ideas through the standard Think, Pair, Share, followed by discussion with teacher-designed questions to consolidate understanding. At the time I felt like the best teacher in the world, but now I see it differently.

Now that we have a decent overview of the various aspects of teaching and learning, we can consider how to build a policy which supports staff to ensure that they are maximising lesson time without becoming too draconian.

Principles vs practices

I have carefully chosen the word principles to describe how we will build the teaching and learning vision for our department. Schools often crave consistency within all they do. This is built on the fundamental idea that there is a 'best way' of doing things – if only there was! It would mean that there would be no long-running debates or arguments, no need to purchase hundreds of books and buy into each educational fad as it rears its forked-tongued head. In an aim to create a cookie-cutter department to please our line managers, we often accidentally create several issues for our staff:

- We try to make them all teach in the exact same way, which might not suit their personality or natural strengths.

- We prioritise resources over techniques. We look at *how* it is done instead of considering *why* in more detail.

- We remove an aspect of intellectualism from the profession, which, in the long run, reduces autonomy, agency and ultimately wellbeing.

Professional autonomy is valued by teachers. Research suggests that staff who are given autonomy report greater job satisfaction and retention within the profession.[13] They are professionals who see themselves as able to fulfil the needs of their students if left to their own devices.

13 J. Worth and J. Van den Brande, *Teacher Autonomy: How Does It Relate to Job Satisfaction and Retention?* (Slough: National Foundation for Educational Research, 2020). Available at: https://tdtrust.org/wp-content/uploads/2020/01/teacher_autonomy_how_does_it_relate_to_job_satisfaction_and_retention.pdf.

However, we must also be honest and admit that we often find a huge variation in the quality of teaching within a school. We also need to be able to support teachers, so that they do not have to discover the best strategies for themselves, as this can be time-consuming and cumbersome. To solve these competing issues, we need to find a way to embody the best ideas with the strongest chance of success, but without forcing a particular approach. Matthew Benyohai likens this to the difference between quality assurance and quality control.[14] Quality assurance will be discussed in detail in Chapter 4 but, put simply, it is all about securing the necessary benchmark of quality but allowing the process by which you get there to look different. Quality control, in contrast, is all about ensuring that each person follows an agreed process. Another way of looking at this is imagining home-baked cookies vs factory-made biscuits. Factory-made biscuits need quality control, whereas home-baked cookies probably just need quality assurance.

We need to be confident that all staff in our department have access to effective strategies that embody the principles that we are looking for, but we do not want to insist that they follow a specific practice if they have their own techniques that achieve the same aim. We need to agree on our principles for great teaching and then provide strategies and resources to support staff to exemplify those principles in action. The converse of this is also true. If they do not have a suitable strategy then we need to have one ready to give them to ensure all students are given the best chance to learn.

Principles for great teaching

Don't reinvent the wheel: a lot of work has already been carried out on various approaches to learning. In my opinion, the best place to start is with Barak Rosenshine's Principles of Instruction. This is a brilliant piece of work for several reasons:

1   It is highly generalisable to all subjects.

2   It dovetails well with the findings from cognitive science that we looked at in Table 1.

3   It is available as a free PDF.[15]

It is not my place to tell you what your principles should be. I don't know your context or the external agendas of your school's senior leadership. Some schools need a highly detailed set of principles, whereas others just need overall themes. In Table 2 I've

---

14 M. Benyohai, Principles and Practices: Is There a Difference and Should We Care? *Medium* [blog] (20 August 2019). Available at: https://medium.com/@mrbenyohai/principles-and-practices-9561a2999ffb.

15 B. Rosenshine, Principles of Instruction: Research Based Strategies That All Teachers Should Know, *American Educator* (Spring 2012): 12–19, 39. Available at: https://www.aft.org/sites/default/files/periodicals/Rosenshine.pdf.

illustrated a couple of principles that we follow in my department so you can see how I have tried to communicate them in a way that supports staff without being too prescriptive. I've chosen two very different examples to show how each column might look in different scenarios.

Table 2: Examples of some teaching principles

Principle	Rationale	Guidance	Resource
Keeping the science the main thing	Students will remember what they think about. Seductive details can derail a student's thoughts and reduce learning.	Try to avoid activities which build engagement through entertainment. The content should be king. Keep explanations short and clear with examples and non-examples. Practicals and demonstrations should have the learning outcome at their heart, not awe and wonder.	CPD training presentation from September.
Regular retrieval practice	Reviewing previously taught material helps encode it into students' long-term memories. It takes advantage of the testing effect, spaced practice and interleaving.	Most lessons should start with a simple low-stakes quiz on prior content. Teachers should review and reteach areas of common weakness.	Retrieval roulette spreadsheets are available for all units.

The aim here is to provide resources which support your principles but leave space for staff to develop or use other approaches if they wish. These principles can become the foundation of your CPD throughout the year and the basis of the common language you use during learning walks or other performance feedback.

Routines: the secret to successful lessons

A large portion of teacher CPD is devoted to task design and explanations, but they are not the most important things to have in place for a successful lesson. Routines are everything in teaching. They establish efficient and effective processes that prevent time being wasted. They also create a culture that builds momentum and compliance. Unlike the principles for great teaching and learning, routines should be as ubiquitous and consistent as possible. Ideally some will be whole school, but that is probably out of your control. At the very least you can control your area of responsibility. However, what are the best routines? Well, that might be up for debate but for me the most extensive book on routines is Doug Lemov's *Teach Like a Champion 2.0*.[16] It is based on best practice from the USA and the techniques for routines are well thought-out and, most importantly, highly practicable. Deliberate practice is a crucial part of teacher development and one which is often ignored. We will discuss this in more detail in Chapter 5.

Classroom routines are worth drilling to perfection. Every minute shaved off a common procedure by embedding routines in September is hours of extra learning time throughout the year. Furthermore, by automating and standardising the routine to be followed by the class, the teacher does not need to devote so much effort and attention to deciding how tasks should be completed; they can devote more thought to monitoring compliance and troubleshooting. Students like routines and it can create a sense of belonging within a group if they share certain rituals. This is very apparent in viral videos from schools in China where classmates come together to learn choreographed dances and exercise. The West often mistakenly thinks that individualism is a child's primary aim, but if you watch groups of children, you can see that they have a deep-seated need to belong. Jonathan Haidt refers to this as humans' 'hive-ish nature':

> people need to lose themselves occasionally by becoming part of an emergent social organism in order to reach the highest levels of human flourishing.[17]

16 D. Lemov, *Teach Like a Champion 2.0: 62 Techniques That Put Students on the Path to College* (San Francisco, CA: Jossey-Bass, 2015).

17 J. Haidt, J. Patrick Seder and S. Kesebir, Hive Psychology, Happiness, and Public Policy, *Journal of Legal Studies*, 37(2) (2008): 113–156 at 113.

Classroom routines are not just limited to having efficient ways of handing out mini whiteboards or books; they permeate the actual mechanics of teaching. Questioning, classroom circulation and teacher explanation also massively benefit from consistent routines.

Table 3 lists common routines from *Teach Like a Champion 2.0*, from my own experience and from years of observing others. I've tried to give a brief description of each technique and explain why it is valuable. Again, each classroom and teacher will have their own priorities and systems, so please don't think of this as an exhaustive list or a directive; it is just here to help you clarify your own thinking.

Table 3: A list of useful routines to use in lessons

Part of lesson	Name of routine	Description	Rationale
Start of lesson	Threshold	Teacher stands on the threshold of the doorway and welcomes students into the class.	Creates a calm start and demonstrates ownership of the classroom. It makes it easy to deal with issues like uniform before the lesson starts.
	Collecting equipment from stations, or the 'buffet approach'	Students take the same route as they enter the room to collect their books and any other equipment, which is always stored in the same place.	Student autonomy provides time for the teacher to focus on setting up the lesson. They can also track the students and narrate positive behaviour.
	Monitors	Each row or group has a monitor to collect and distribute specific equipment.	Less intense than the buffet approach but takes up more time in the lesson.
	Do-now starter	A staple in most schools, all lessons start with a similar formatted task, often involving retrieval practice.	As students enter they know what to do without having to be told. Teachers can focus on the slow starters, take the register, etc.

Part of lesson	Name of routine	Description	Rationale
During the lesson	Signal, pause, insist	An explicit and consistent routine to establish silence. Use a verbal (and possibly also a visual) signal for silence (e.g. counting down), followed by waiting for silence.	Although it is boring for the teacher due to its repetitiveness, students need to be very clear about what they are expected to do. This clarity ensures that it is easy to pick up the students who are not paying attention or choosing to disobey.
	Cold call	Pose a question to all students, allow time for the students to think and then choose one student to answer.	By not addressing the student by name until after the question, all students think they might be asked, so they all have to think of an answer. This improves the amount of thinking in the class.
	No opt out	When a student answers a question by saying 'I don't know', ask another student and then go back to the original student once the correct answer has been offered. Get them to repeat it. Ask them the same question multiple times in the next few lessons.	Students often claim ignorance because they don't want to make a mistake. By using 'no opt out', students are held accountable. Students who do not know also get multiple chances to embed the right answer.
	Turn and talk	Use a hand gesture or verbal cue to demonstrate when students should turn and talk to their partner.	Paired discussion is a powerful tool that improves students' thinking and their confidence to answer questions.

Part of lesson	Name of routine	Description	Rationale
	Turn and talk (cont.)	Accompany this with a verbal time limit.	Imposing a short, punchy time limit can really increase the feeling of pace in a lesson. Often talk-time goes on for too long. By having a clear cue, you can build in your expectations without having to re-explain the rules each time.
	Brighten lines	Ensure that changes in activities are perceived clearly by making the beginnings and endings of activities visible and crisp.	When changing activities, it is vital that there are clear boundaries of when one task stops and the next one begins. Before the students are allowed to begin the task, ensure that you tell them: what they are to do (mode of participation), how long they have to do it (clear time limits), and how you will check completion (mode of response). Before setting a task, always use questions to check that students can repeat the instructions back to you. Spending one minute brightening the lines means you don't spend five minutes re-explaining everything to each table.

Part of lesson	Name of routine	Description	Rationale
	Tracking not watching	Be deliberate about how you look around your classroom. Decide what you're looking for and remain disciplined in the face of distractions.	When you are monitoring your students, are you making the most of that time? Are you checking their progress? Helping those who are stuck? By keeping a note of who's offered good responses and who's struggling, you can orchestrate a follow-up discussion and tasks to ensure that all benefit.
	Corners then circulate	Once the task is set, move to one corner of the room so you can see everyone.	Too often, teachers get sucked in by the first struggling student they see. Instead, view the room and judge the level of success. If you see lots of students struggling, stop and reframe the task or add scaffolding. If most are on-task, begin your circulation.
	Circulation route	Create a route that allows you to visit all the students in the classroom in an efficient manner.	Too often, teachers rush from hand to hand and quiet or competent students slip through the net. To get a better idea of how students are performing you need to circulate. If a student needs help, feel free to go to them but return to the route so that everyone gets seen.

Part of lesson	Name of routine	Description	Rationale
	Keep your face to the class	Like a referee, you need to be able to see all the players at all times. Make sure to angle your body when helping a student, so you can still see most of the class with a glance.	Students need to know that they can be seen and will more easily drift off task if you have your back to them. This links in with circulation and tracking not watching.
End of lesson	Packing away	This will essentially be the opposite of your start of lesson routine, but don't think that it will enable the students to do it adequately without practice.	How do you want the books stored? Remember, how this class puts the glue sticks away directly affects how the next class treats them. This is all about clarity and standards: the two drivers of improvement in performance.
	Setting homework	Ensure that the class is silent and listening. Explain where they will find the homework (e.g. online or on a hand-out) and how it fits into the current learning journey.	If homework is valued, there needs to be a formal way of ensuring that all students are told about it. Students will do homework to avoid getting in trouble, but if they know it has a purpose and has not been set 'just because' then the quality of the work will be higher. You need to deliver a sales pitch that convinces them to spend time thinking about your subject outside the classroom. It could be done during any part of the lesson.

Part of lesson	Name of routine	Description	Rationale
	Orderly dismissal	Get the students to leave the classroom in a calm and orderly fashion.	Do you get them to stand behind their seats? Do you dismiss row by row? This will be dependent on your situation, but one thing is for sure and it is that orderly dismissal is an important step in ensuring that students enter their next class calmly. You are helping your fellow teachers by setting high expectations in your classroom.

Student motivation

In this chapter we have taken a broad pass through cognitive science, theories of knowledge acquisition, and activities that seem to provide the best chance of students acquiring said knowledge. Unfortunately, these aspects are not the biggest barrier to our students' learning; the students themselves are. A student's own motivation is hugely important. A well-motivated student can thrive in any school environment; conversely, even in the best schools there are students who appear to be immune to the school's Midas touch. This universal truth is weaved into our culture through the idiom 'You can take a horse to water, but you cannot make it drink.' In the high-stakes world of school accountability this is shown in the difference in outcomes of various cohorts. National data shows that certain minority ethnic groups considerably outperform white British students.[18] A 2015

18 Department for Education, GCSE results ('Attainment 8') (22 August 2019). Available at: https://www.ethnicity-facts-figures.service.gov.uk/education-skills-and-training/11-to-16-years-old/gcse-results-attainment-8-for-children-aged-14-to-16-key-stage-4/latest#by-ethnicity.

Department for Education report into the outcomes of different ethnic groups experiencing deprivation alludes to the impact of cultural factors:

> **Schools also have an important role in raising attainment, although the evidence suggests the relative contribution of schools is smaller than that of parental, family and student factors.[19]**

The simple truth is if we cannot effectively motivate our students, no matter their background, it will not matter how much time and energy we put into our own practice; students will not progress through the curriculum effectively. Historically, motivation was viewed from a purely behaviourist point of view: students are motivated by their desire for rewards and their dislike of punishments. Much like the adage of the carrot and the stick, it is just an issue of finding the right carrot and the right stick to get the job done.

More recently we have begun to understand just how murky the idea of using incentives and deterrents to influence motivation is. Consider the Californian attendance experiment conducted by Carly D. Robinson et al.[20] In 2015 they set up a study involving over 15,000 schoolchildren. Their theory was that if they used preannounced rewards – telling the students that if they achieve 100% this term, they will receive an award – then students' attendance would rise. They compared this to a surprise award – one given with no prior knowledge. To their surprise, they found that the preannounced award made no difference to attendance. The reward was not valuable enough to force a change in behaviour, or, to put it another way, the juice was not worth the squeeze. What was even more surprising was what happened to the students who received the surprise award: their attendance dropped the following term. The researchers theorise that in giving an award, you also send the message that the student is above your expectations. This allows them to justify a day off as being 'owed' to them next term.

So, if rewards and sanctions are not the straightforward solutions we once hoped they would be, what can we do to motivate our students? Enter Gabrielle Garon-Carrier et al., who investigated the link between motivation in maths at age 7 and performance later in

19 L. Stokes, H. Rolfe, N. Hudson Sharp and S. Stevens, *A Compendium of Evidence on Ethnic Minority Resilience to the Effects of Deprivation on Attainment: Research Report.* Ref: DFE-RR439A (London: Department for Education, 2015), p. 7. Available at: https://assets.publishing.service.gov.uk/government/uploads/system/uploads/attachment_data/file/439861/RR439A-Ethnic_minorities_and_attainment_the_effects_of_poverty.pdf.

20 C. D. Robinson, J. Gallus, M. G. Lee and T. Rogers, The Demotivating Effect (and Unintended Message) of Awards, *Organizational Behavior and Human Decision Processes* (2019). DOI: 10.1016/j.obhdp.2019.03.006. Available at: https://scholar.harvard.edu/files/todd_rogers/files/the_demotivating_effect_and_unintended_message_of_awards_vf_01.pdf.

participants' school careers.[21] They found that while intrinsic motivation did not correlate to improved performance, performance at age 7 did correlate to motivation in later years. Put simply, students like to feel competent, so devote their time to things that provide that feeling. If we can breed success in our students by ensuring that they can perform in lessons, then we can create a positive feedback loop of motivation and success. When I led Key Stage 5, every year I carried out a survey of students' opinions of their subjects and teachers. When collating the results there was always a clear trend: in subjects that scored highly, the most common praise was a variant of 'When I am stuck, they help me to get unstuck.' It's the defining feature of a good teacher and speaks to the idea that competence is motivational.

Now we have considered these important aspects of teaching and learning, we can see how they fit together. By understanding the structures of knowledge, we can see the value of cognitive science. By using cognitive science's recommendations, we can create lessons which enable a change in long-term memory and a feeling of competence. This competence breeds motivation, so students will hopefully apply themselves to tasks with greater effort.

Recap

- Learning is a change in long-term memory.

- This means that learning happens over time and not only in the classroom.

- Cognitive science does not provide a silver bullet but does provide best bets for supporting learning.

- Leading teaching and learning is about identifying and exemplifying principles and allowing the freedom to adapt them to a teacher's way of working.

- Routines should provide calm and efficient classroom environments.

- Motivation and attention are important if students are to learn, so we should do our best to create climates in which both are encouraged.

---

21 G. Garon-Carrier, M. Boivin, F. Guay, Y. Kovas, G. Dionne and J. P. Lemelin et al., Intrinsic Motivation and Achievement in Mathematics in Elementary School: A Longitudinal Investigation of their Association, *Child Development*, 87(1) (2016): 165–175.

Reflect

- What are my principles for teaching and learning?
- Do my principles align with the evidence?
- Do my current schemes of work encourage these principles?
- Where do I need to insist on certain practices and where can I afford a degree of flexibility?
- Which resources would support all my staff in adopting my principles?
- Which routines do I want to be ubiquitous in my department?
- Are there any subject-specific routines that need to be considered?

Chapter 3

Leading assessment

Not all numbers are the same, and they don't always mean what you might think.

Richard Selfridge[1]

Assessment is a bit of a false idol in education. We can tend to trust assessment data much more than we should. To a certain degree it makes sense. Just like the ancient Mayans would gain solace from believing that the quality of their harvest was due to their devotion to Hun Hunahpu, the god of maize, teachers place their trust in their assessment data. This is because they are either unaware of the complex interactions between a multitude of factors which have contributed to a certain test score on a certain day, or simply because it makes life easier. Let me be clear, I am not saying that 'teachers trust test data because they are stupid', more that teachers trust test data because it is convenient and provides them with a sense of certainty and comfort. In much the same way as Mayan nobles would willingly perform bloodletting rituals, teachers will self-flagellate themselves with mountains of marking and question level analysis in an attempt to provide a feeling of control in a world ruled by mysterious forces that are largely beyond their control.

We feel this way because education is, by definition, a complex problem. Complex problems, or 'wicked issues', are those with which there is little to no:[2]

- Agreement on the definition of the problem, owing to multiple values, perceptions and perspectives.

- Clear solutions to the problem, owing to the wide array of possible solutions and trade-offs associated with each.

- Easily identified causes or authorities, due to the problem having multiple potential causes, jurisdictions, stakeholders and regulators, and implications.

It is easy to read that list and see why educational impact is so hard to quantify. Assessment has a difficult challenge to overcome.

---

1   See https://www.databustingforschools.co.uk/.
2   H. W. J. Rittel and M. M. Webber, Dilemmas in a General Theory of Planning, *Policy Sciences*, 4 (1973): 155–169.

Assessment theory

Assessment theory is a complex area of expertise – one that, quite frankly, I was only aware of at a surface level when I began planning this book. Fortunately, I am lucky enough to call Deep Singh Ghataura a friend. Deep has an incredible level of expertise in assessment theory and he is also a science teacher. Through our countless discussions we have tried to take the most relevant aspects of assessment theory, break them down and exemplify them so you can understand not only the range of choices you have, but also the consequences of each option.

In my experience, very few teachers and leaders *really* understand assessment. Until recently I would have counted myself in their number. There are plenty of professionals who understand the process of assessment and how to use spreadsheets to analyse data and create pivot tables and pie charts, etc. But that is not an understanding of assessment. To understand assessment, you need to be aware of the challenges that occur in measurement and the limitations *created by* the choices you make. There is no perfect assessment or assessment system. We must instead understand the choices we make and their consequences. Early in my career, assessment was like something out of the fable of the emperor's new clothes.

I vividly remember this conversation from my third year of teaching. 'Come on, Adam! You predicted they were going to get a C and they got a D – that's not on! If we had known they were working at a D grade, we could have put them into the intervention sessions and got them over the line. In future, please don't inflate students' predictions. We won't judge you; we just need to know.'

The problem was, I thought that they were going to get a C grade. They had got one in the last topic test, and their target was a C, so I thought that they would get one in the exam. Unfortunately for me, this was a piece of 'drive-by feedback' (see Chapter 8 for more on this), so I didn't get a chance to explain my rationale. Coming from a biochemistry background, I was always confused by the certainty with which teachers talked about 'levels of progress' and 'targets vs predictions'. However, it was so ubiquitous at the time, you just assume that everyone knows something you don't and before long you are parroting back the same faulty rationale during conversations.

In this chapter we will vindicate past me and explain why it was not my fault that I got the prediction wrong. Not that I'm bitter or anything.

Validity and reliability

Let's start with looking at one test score. A student, let's call them Lara, takes a test and scores 54. What does that tell us? Not much, obviously.

If we know that the test is out of 100, it tells us a bit more. If we know how the rest of the class did, it tells us a little bit about how she performed compared to her peers. If the test was, say, sat by an entire year, we learn even more. If the test was sat by the entire nation, we would have an idea about how good Lara is relative to the rest of the country.

What if we knew which questions she got right? Would we then know what she does and doesn't know? Well, this is where it gets a bit messy. Let's take a step back and recognise an elephant in the room: the choices you make about how and when you assess students will greatly impact the outcomes of the assessment. This is complicated further by the subject being assessed; some subjects are just much easier to assess than others. When it comes to evaluating assessment, you are really judging it on its *validity* and its *reliability*. To ensure clarity, let's define those terms.

Validity is the degree to which the assessment measures the thing it is intended to measure. For example, if a reading test is printed in an incredibly small font, it has reduced validity as those students who are visually impaired will not be able to access it. Similarly, a test might be very good at assessing a student's music knowledge, but if it is not aligned with the GCSE specification, it will have low validity as a predictor of GCSE performance. Validity is not a property of the assessment itself; it is more a property of the conclusions you attempt to draw from the results. Validity, it appears, is in the eye of the beholder.

Reliability does not consider intent. It is a measure of how consistent the results of the test are. Would the same student be able to get a similar score if the test was taken again? This is sometimes called replicability. Would they get an equivalent score on a similar test? This is sometimes called reproducibility. For an assessment to be reliable we need to accomplish two things: firstly, we need to be able to mark the test correctly without ambiguity (inter-rater reliability[3]) and, secondly, we need the test to be able to distinguish between students of different abilities. When it comes to inter-rater reliability, nothing beats a well-constructed multiple-choice question. There is no ambiguity. Closely behind are the numerical questions. Some wiggle room has crept in but, at the end of the day, 10.4 is 10.4 (to one decimal place), so marking is quite easy. To ensure performance accuracy we need to make sure that the questions are of an appropriate challenge so that students with a broad range of abilities score a broad range of marks.

---

3   Inter-rater reliability is the degree at which raters (in this case markers of the tests) agree on the score of an individual test script.

You always see the term 'a good discriminator' in examiners' reports as code for 'this question was hard and only the best got it right'. You need a balance of questions: simple enough to make it accessible for the lowest performers, but also challenging enough for the highest performers. If many students get 100% in your assessment, it's probably a bit too easy. When it comes to reliability, some subjects are more naturally suited to highly reliable assessments – for example, maths.

But what about English?

To make English assessment as reliable as possible, we should use multiple-choice questions. In fact, in some countries this is regularly done – for example, the American SAT has a large grammar and comprehension section that uses multiple-choice questions extensively to assess aspects of the English curriculum. When we consider the validity of the English assessment, we could make the case that English needs to have a large amount of free-response questions in which students produce extended written answers, as that kind of assessment more closely mirrors the aims of the curriculum. By assessing in this style, though, we must accept that there is a cost to the test's reliability. Marking extended essay answers is incredibly difficult and can be highly subjective. Even with training there will be variance that is unavoidable. So, it came as no surprise when a 2018 study by the British exam regulator Ofqual found that grading accuracy in A-level maths was at 96% but English literature was as low as 52%.[4] This sounds horrific, but it is a function of the desire to create an assessment with integrity to the values of the course. So, our choices in how we structure assessments have implications on what we can infer from the outcomes.

We must be careful not to confuse the debate on the ontology of our subject – the nature of what our subject is – with the issues with its metrology – how we measure students' performance. We do have to be aware that certain ontological decisions will favour different assessment styles. It is important when designing our assessments that we are clear exactly how we view the nature of our subject and accept that this will have consequences for the assessment methods we choose.[5]

---

4   S. Rhead, B. Black and A. Pinot de Moira, *Marking Consistency Metrics: An Update*. Ref: Ofqual/18/6449/2 (Coventry: Ofqual, 2018). Available at: https://assets.publishing.service.gov.uk/government/uploads/system/uploads/attachment_data/file/759207/Marking_consistency_metrics_-_an_update_-_FINAL64492.pdf.

5   D. Wiliam, What Counts as Evidence of Educational Achievement? The Role of Constructs in the Pursuit of Equity in Assessment, *Review of Research in Education*, 34(1) (2010): 254–284.

Aggregation is our friend

Let's go back to poor Lara and her score of 54. We now realise that the subject and the nature of the assessment also play a role in the amount of trust we can place in her result when it comes to awarding her a grade. Let's make it simple and say that Lara sat a maths test and scored 54. To help, let's specify that it was a trigonometry test. Now we can focus on what that means for Lara's performance. One of the most powerful tools we have to improve assessment is aggregation. This can come in two forms: aggregating scores over time and aggregating content in the form of synoptic assessment.

If we aggregate scores over time, then we get a picture of that student's performance compared to their baseline. In our example, let's say Lara has an average test score over the last year of 44. Now, can we say that she is better at trigonometry than her other topics? At first glance it appears so. But what if I told you that the class average on this test was 60? Does that change your opinion of her performance? Now, what if I told you the aggregated class average up to this test was 46? Again, our ideas change. Some topics are inherently harder than others. With this data we can say that Lara is generally average for the class in maths, she scored more marks in this test than she typically does, but this test was slightly easier than the others she has sat. Or is this good news? It might mean that this topic was taught better and so students have really grasped it. Well done! We don't know that yet, but it could be! How can we find out? Well, we can make sure our whole cohort sits the same series of assessments. Then we can look at differences between classes and at how similar students have performed. Only then will we start to get a greater understanding of how Lara is really doing.

Curriculum backwash

What if I use the same test with different classes over the course of a few years? Now I will have historical data that I can use for comparisons. I might even be able to draw comparisons between performance in this test and performance in national exams, like GCSEs.

There is, however, one issue with reusing the same assessment: curriculum backwash. In her talk at researchED Durrington and in her follow-up blog, Professor Becky Allen discussed a number of issues around standardised testing and judging student progress.[6]

---

6   B. Allen, What If We Cannot Measure Pupil Progress? *Becky Allen: Musings on Education Policy* [blog] (23 May 2018). Available at: https://rebeccaallen.co.uk/2018/05/23/what-if-we-cannot-measure-pupil-progress/.

One of the most important was the idea that using such testing subconsciously creates a pressure on the curriculum. The teacher marking the test pays attention to the mistakes made due to lack of familiarity with the questions, content or examples, and when teaching it the following year they introduce those specific examples to increase the students' familiarity. This kind of teaching to the test is more apparent when performance management targets and reporting cycles increase the stakes of the results, but even in a low-stakes environment this backwash will occur inadvertently.

Assessment is a fickle friend, it seems.

What can we do then?

We need to give Lara an indication of how she is doing, and we need to report to her parents. All analytical approaches are imperfect; however, there are some powerful statistical models available that claim to tell you, quite accurately, how students are performing. One such example is the Rasch model, which compares a student's answer to the probability of them getting it correct.[7] It is not for the faint-hearted and it requires whole-cohort individual question data to be input. If you want to get measurable progression information and are willing to put the time in to collect the data, this is your best bet.

At the level below, but still requiring some statistical hard graft, is the work of Matthew Benyohai.[8] He uses bee swarm plots to show where an individual student's score puts them within the distribution of the class or cohort by using standardised scores, or Z scores, for that test. This allows you to see where a student sits within a cohort, with progression for that student being defined as an increase in the standard score.

What about those of us who aren't comfortable with that level of analysis? Well, there are some simple things that can really help to paint a picture of the student's result in context. Ranking students, while somewhat crude, gives students and parents useful information in a form that they understand. Providing a change in rank also helps them to see a simple trajectory. The year average is also a helpful guide, or, if you set your classes by ability, a class average might also help.

---

7   C. Granger, Rasch Analysis Is Important to Understand and Use for Measurement, *Rasch Measurement Transactions*, 21(3) (2008): 1122–1123. Available at: https://www.rasch.org/rmt/rmt213d.htm.

8   M. Benyohai, The Difference Between Measuring Progress and Attainment, *Medium* [blog] (7 June 2018). Available at: https://medium.com/@mrbenyohai/the-difference-between-measuring-progress-and-attainment-7269a41cdd8.

Here are some quick tips for ranking to help you if you have never done such a thing:

- Data needs to be complete and on time. Absent students need to sit the test ASAP. Missing data causes huge changes in rank unnecessarily.

- Tiers of entry can cause issues. If you have two tiers, you can combine them and rank based on common content, or you can produce two ranks: one for each tier. Students with identical scores will get the same rank, and the next rank will be the number of that result if the previous ranks were not identical. For example, if two students get the same score for second place, it will go 1, 2, 2, 4 not 1, 2, 2, 3.

- If displaying publicly, the bottom ten students do not have their names displayed, just their ID number.

- The bottom two students are fictional and have random ID numbers. No student is bottom.

- Avoid displaying any other data apart from scores and ranks. No classes, no teachers, etc. That is just asking for trouble.

Awarding grades

So far, we have not awarded a grade. This is where I might get really annoying. I would argue that whatever grade you award, it is going to be unreliable and I hope that I have explained my points well enough that you agree. Grades are the product of large-scale, synoptic terminal assessments. GCSEs, for example, comprise multiple hours' worth of questions which cover most of the specification. Lara did a test on trigonometry. If we give her a grade 4 for trigonometry, what are we saying? There are three possibilities:

1   If you sat a GCSE that was 100% trigonometry, you would score a grade 4.

2   Students that score this many marks in trigonometry go on to score a grade 4 in GCSE maths.

3   You sit at the point of normal distribution where grade 4 is most often awarded.

This is the crux of the problem. When awarding a grade to a student, different teachers mean different things. The question becomes: does your line manager know what you mean when you award a grade? Is there an agreement within your school? If you are not clear with them and your A is their B, then there is a chance for a significant misunderstanding. As leaders we need to ensure that however we decide to build our assessment model we are clear with everyone what we are trying to achieve.

Building an assessment system

Now that we have a greater appreciation of the implications of our assessment choices on the data it generates, we can see that some things are favoured over others:

- Longer, more synoptic tests are better than shorter topic tests, as they provide aggregation of content.

- Question style should closely match the aims of the curriculum, but this might affect marking reliability.

- We should keep in mind issues with our subject context when awarding grades.

- Reporting where students sit within the cohort via rank or another means can be helpful.

- Tests should be reviewed periodically to prevent curriculum backwash.

How these ideas are applied will vary greatly. Things like your reporting cycle and logistical issues like venue availability all play a role.

Here's how I would do it:

- Have two testing windows: January and July.

- The test in January takes half the time of the July one and samples all content from September to Christmas. The July test samples the entire year's content and vital prior content from previous years.

- The marks are used to report attainment to parents twice a year, along with rank within the cohort, thus you can also compare any changes in rank from January to July. Estimated grades can be awarded in a multitude of ways, but the best is probably to look at a distribution of scores for the whole cohort and compare it to a national distribution of grades for a particular subject. If the cohort is around the national average, then the middle of the bell curve will be within the grade 4–5 area. Then work out towards the edges.

In the humanities and English, where we know the integrity of the assessment makes the accuracy lower, we might offer some different strategies. Mark schemes and exemplar work to illustrate each grade will help. The key component to increasing the reliability of these judgements is to increase the number of judgements made on each piece of work. Double and triple marking have both been proven to increase the reliability of the grading of English essays, but at a time cost.[9] The easiest way to strike a balance is to incorporate standardisation and moderation. By standardising an initial sample, teachers can discuss any issues before they begin the bulk of the marking. This is how exam boards mark terminal exams. After the scripts are marked, moderation begins. This allows for double marking a sample, including examples of each grade awarded. Daisy Christodoulou and the team at No More Marking offer tools for the effective use of comparative judgement.[10] They claim that people are much better at comparing two pieces of work than they are applying detailed criteria. So, by comparing samples of work it is possible to rank the essays and then divide the marks appropriately. This achieves the same aim as double marking, as it increases the number of judgements each paper receives.

Question level analysis

Question level analysis is a process carried out on a recently completed set of marked papers. By collating the individual marks scored in each question by each student, you can perform a sort of post-mortem on the strengths and weaknesses of the cohort or individual student. Question level analysis is commonplace. The idea is that if we forensically analyse students' performance in a recent assessment, we can identify gaps in their understanding, patch them up and have confidence that they will perform better in the next exam. Unfortunately, this is built on a simple assumption that is incorrect: that a student who understands the concept gets the question right. This seems obvious, but as Professor Rob Coe illustrates in his blog for CEM:

> In a naïve understanding of assessment, students either know it or they don't: if they do then they should get the question right, if they don't then they shouldn't. But the reality is captured by this smooth curve, the ICC [item characteristic curve], that shows how the probability gradually increases with 'ability'. If your knowledge is such that you have an 80% chance of a correct answer, then one time in five you will get that question wrong.[11]

9   T. Benton and T. Gallacher, Is Comparative Judgement Just a Quick Form of Multiple Marking? *Research Matters*, 22 (Autumn 2018): 22–28. Available at: https://www.cambridgeassessment.org.uk/Images/514987-is-comparative-judgement-just-a-quick-form-of-multiple-marking-.pdf.

10 https://www.nomoremarking.com/aboutUs2.

11 R. Coe, Why Assessment May Tell You Less Than You Think – Part I, *CEM Blog* [blog] (21 November 2018). Available at: https://www.cem.org/blog/why-assessment-may-tell-you-less-than-you-think-part-1.

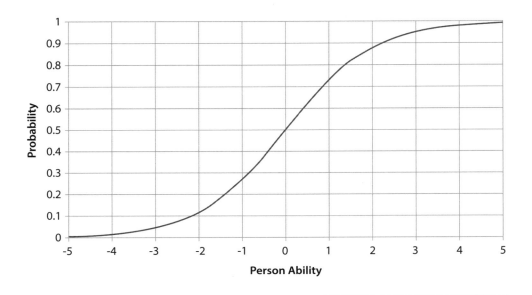

This is akin to the app that predicts the weather on your phone. If there is an 80% chance of rain, it does not mean that there will be rain 80% of the time; it means that if you were to live this day multiple times, four in five days you would see rain. While Professor Coe's certainty regarding a students' 'ability' is not something that I would be willing to hang my hat on, the idea that each student has an individual probability of scoring a mark is an important one. Our question level analysis can tell us something, but it might not offer a full picture of what a student can and can't do. Once this is understood, the idea that a student's question level analysis will be valid looks shaky. This is compounded further by variations in assessment objectives. Given that most subjects overlay assessment objectives within different contexts, it creates another problem for question level analysis. Did the student get this wrong because they lack the knowledge of medieval medicine or because they are bad at using secondary sources? The fact that they scored 3 out of 10 does not make that distinction for us. There is also the question of the time and effort involved in collating the question level data and analysing it. To some, this time is not worth the pay-off.

This is not to say that we shouldn't use assessments to infer gaps in our students' understanding; however, a much more effective way is to do this holistically. When marking papers, simply take note of the common and frustrating mistakes noticed. This avoids wasting time going through the papers in detail, but allows you to design activities which can be used to practise those areas of weakness.

The workload element

After all this thought and organising we have one final thing to consider: the people involved. There is a significant workload implication with any assessment system. Topic tests create regular small amounts of marking and data entry. Larger end-of-term tests can create bottlenecks that erode staff morale. The most important thing is to explain your rationale and, most importantly, do not try to do every form of assessment! More is not always better.

Final thoughts

Assessment is a tricky thing to get right. Most people don't understand it and think that it is more accurate than it really is. Even though it is flawed, assessment is also vital. It is vital to the students more than to the teachers. Students need to experience formal testing relatively regularly. This reduces their exam anxiety as they become accustomed to the emotions involved. It provides a version of exposure therapy that helps prepare them for terminal assessments.

Ultimately, assessment data is only valuable if we understand the context in which it was gathered. More importantly, we need to ensure that those who line manage us are aware of the limitations of our data. (Ideas for managing up will be covered in Chapter 8.) I think that understanding assessment is a very unnerving process; the more you know, the more you realise you don't really know anything for certain. At least now we can agree that when I wrongly predicted a C to a student who then got a D it wasn't my fault! I mean, I was naive to interpret the data that way, but it was also hard to make the prediction more accurately than I did. It is a function of the exam system that some students must get a D. I'm sure that we can both sleep better now that we know I was right all along.

Assessment decisions by design

To support you in your assessment decisions I have tried to summarise the different aspects that you'll need to consider. The aim is to help you to make these decisions with the outcomes you want in mind.

Table 4: Evaluating different threads of assessment

Thread of assessment	Aspect	Advantages	Limitations
Mode of response	Multiple-choice question	Easy to mark. Can be fully automated. Good at informing you of highly specific aspects of understanding and identifying misconceptions.	Writing good distractors is hard. Students will not be able to demonstrate depth and breadth of understanding. Personal insights and conclusions are not possible. Possible literacy barrier.
	Extended response/essay	Valid inferences can be made if you are interested in a student's ability to convey meaning within your subject. Students can demonstrate depth and breadth of understanding.	Low inter-rater reliability leads to reduced grade certainty. This can be reduced by introducing double marking. Labour-intensive to mark. Requires moderation.

Thread of assessment	Aspect	Advantages	Limitations
	Short answer	Well suited for aspects of most subjects in which you are aiming to judge a student's understanding of a particular skill or concept. Generally high marking accuracy if mark schemes are well produced and clearly define the range of accepted answers.	Not always possible to assess the entire domain; sampling will often be needed. If not carefully constructed, the students will not produce work that is detailed enough to infer valid conclusions about their understanding.
	Performance	Good at judging a student's ability to perform a series of tasks or skills. Students can demonstrate a range of understanding and be assessed holistically. Formative feedback can be verbal, instant and precise, resulting in rapid improvements.	Not always a priority for all subjects. Needs clear marking criteria, exemplification and moderation. Hard to create assessment criteria that adequately include the entire range of ability, which can lead to reduced inter-rater reliability. Is not able to judge a student's ability over time; it's merely a snapshot. For a group performance, it can be hard to separate the student's individual work from that of the group.

Thread of assessment	Aspect	Advantages	Limitations
	Portfolio	Good at judging a student's ability to perform a series of tasks or skills. Students can demonstrate a range of skills and knowledge and be assessed holistically. Performance is sometimes a crucial aspect of the subject's disciplinary knowledge, so it becomes ontologically important.	Can be time-consuming. It is hard to balance the rigidity required for adequate inter-rater reliability with the freedom of expression some subjects warrant. This can lead to a view that aspects of the portfolio become tick-box activities. Due to the duration of the portfolio construction, it is not always easy to ensure that all students have had access to the same amounts of time and support.
Assessment structure	Synoptic questions	Forces students to apply knowledge from a range of topics. Replicates the approach taken with GCSE and A-level assessments.	Reduces the number of marks available for assessment of current content. Or it might increase the length of the assessment (if current content is included as well).

Thread of assessment	Aspect	Advantages	Limitations
	Including questions from prior topics	Forces students to apply knowledge from a range of topics. Provides anchoring questions to measure changes in performance.	Reduces the number of marks available for assessment of current content. Or it might increase the length of the assessment (if current content is included as well).
	Only covering current content	More marks are available to assess the topic that the students have been studying recently. Allows for more marks to assess each aspect in more detail or via a range of assessment objectives.	Does not encourage review of prior content. Does not encourage the linking of ideas. Has less in common with the most likely structures of GCSE and A-level assessment, which will reduce the validity of the scores.
Assessment organisation	Silo questions by topic	Easier to mark as you do not need to know the whole curriculum. Potentially tells you a student's relative ability in each topic. Test can be administered at any time.	Does not encourage students to think synoptically, so will not encourage them to make links between topics.

Thread of assessment	Aspect	Advantages	Limitations
	Synoptic assessment	Similar to terminal assessment models, so provides high levels of validity. Encourages students to revisit old content and make links.	Harder to mark as you need to know the whole curriculum. Can only be administered once students have covered all the content. Difficult to glean relative ability in each topic.
	High-frequency, low-duration tests	Easy to administer as can fit into a lesson. Disperses staff workload throughout the year. Less stressful for students. More likely to assess the entire domain of the topic.	May not be synoptic. Students will not take it as seriously as stakes are lower.
	Low-frequency, high-duration test	Allows for synoptic assessment. Students are built up for them so prepare better. More in line with terminal assessments at GCSE and A level.	Harder to administer as they are longer than a lesson. Can make students more stressed. Marking needs to be managed carefully. Might not be possible to assess the desired domain completely.

Thread of assessment	Aspect	Advantages	Limitations
Interpreting results	Giving out grades	Students understand them. Parents understand them.	GCSE-type grades are not awardable for partial completion of the course. Hard to assign grades with a degree of certainty.
	Percentages	Easy to understand. Simple to calculate.	If different assessments are varied lengths, it might distort percentages. Non-linear as most students are average, which makes it difficult to judge relative performance. For example, the difference in ability between two students who get 45% and 46% respectively is not the same as two students who get 95% and 96%. Harder to make comparisons between different tests in the same subject.
	Z scores	Harder to calculate. Not well understood by students, parents and possibly even teachers.	Give a greater measure of performance and are standardised to the mean results. Need a sample size of 30+ to provide meaningful data.

Thread of assessment	Aspect	Advantages	Limitations
	Sharing the class average	Allows parents to determine performance relative to the rest of the class.	No information on the spread of results means it can be depressed by absentees or unusually low scores.
	Ranking students	Gives a clear indication of the relative performance of each student.	Has potential to have negative consequences for students' wellbeing. Does not tell you how this cohort compares to previous years. Is dependent on cohort ability.
	Question level analysis	Gives an indication of where marks were scored in that test. Identifies areas for further investigation. Possibly tells you where gaps lie in students' knowledge.	Time-consuming. False degree of certainty. Ignores the role that assessment objectives play in questions.

Table 5: What type of assessment is best for what function?

What do we want assessment to do?	Best bets	Unlikely to help
Set students by performance	Large synoptic tests Ranking Predominantly short-answer or multiple-choice questions	Short, siloed tests Extended response or essay questions Reporting percentages

What do we want assessment to do?	Best bets	Unlikely to help
Find gaps to inform interventions	Short, siloed end-of-topic tests Question level analysis Predominantly short-answer or multiple-choice questions	Long, synoptic tests Extended response or essay questions
Measure progress within a cohort	Long, synoptic tests with common content Ranking Z scores Rasch model	Extended response or essay questions Percentages Raw scores
Assign grades	Long tests with common content Ranking Z scores	Percentages Raw scores
Judge teacher performance	Don't do it	Seriously, don't

Recap

- Assessment is incredibly hard to get right. There are always compromises.

- Assessing students in a valid way sometimes means we have to compromise the reliability of the assessment.

- This is not a problem if we are aware of this limitation and react accordingly.

- Progress is hard to measure but statistical tools can help to make it easier.

- If you do not like statistics, then aggregation, ranking and comparing to cohort averages are easier ways to provide context to students' results.

- Carefully consider your assessment strategy through the lens of how it will impact students and staff as well as how meaningful the results will be.

- Question level analysis can tell you some things, but it might not tell you as much as you hope, so the opportunity cost of collecting and acting on the data should be considered.
- Above all, communicate the limitations of your assessment model to your line management so that they are aware of what the data can and can't say.

Reflection

- What do I want my assessment policy to achieve?
- Does my current policy achieve those goals?
- Am I making valid inferences from the data I am collecting?
- What do I mean when I award grades from my assessments?
- Is my line manager aware of my grading rationale?
- Is my assessment policy generating unnecessary workload for my staff?

Chapter 4
Leading quality assurance

In Chapters 1 to 3 we reviewed the knowledge and skills we want our students to acquire, decided on the best strategies for efficiently transferring the teacher's understanding to the students, and discussed what assessment can and can't tell us. So, now we have our vision for teaching in our department in place, we must decide how we will ensure that each student has the best experience possible.

Quality assurance is used in a wide variety of industries to assess whether each step in a process is being carried out to a desired standard. This is slightly different from quality control, as it allows for variation if overall effectiveness is maintained. In teaching this is incredibly challenging. As mentioned in Chapter 2, teaching is the epitome of a complex problem. As Graham Nuthall wrote in *The Hidden Lives of Learners*:

> **It is also assumed that learning is the more or less automatic result of engaging in classroom activities. If students do what the teacher expects of them, follow the instructions carefully, complete all the aspects of the tasks, then the students will learn what the teacher expects. However, our research shows that almost none of this is true.[1]**

So how do we try to measure something we can't see? Well, we create proxies, things we think indicate that learning is likely to be occurring. Proxies provide us with metrics: things we can measure easily. In theory, if we identify the best proxies and create metrics that are fair, then we will have a quality-assurance programme that will achieve our aims, right?

> **Metric:** A quantifiable measure we can use to track a process.
>
> **Proxies:** Metrics which allow us to infer that a hard-to-measure process is occurring.

I'd love this to be true. I've certainly been in training that pretends it is the truth, and I'm sure that there are many schools and other organisations which assume it is day to day. The inconvenient truth is that these systems often suffer from a number of fatal flaws.

---

1   G. Nuthall, *The Hidden Lives of Learners* (Wellington: NZCER Press, 2007), p. 103.

Determining the quality of teaching is actually incredibly difficult. It might be the hardest thing a leader has to do. In this chapter we will look at some of the proxies commonly used to do this and their suitability for the task. Then we will explore the unintended consequences of turning proxies into metrics. We will conclude by discussing some possible solutions to these problems and how to implement them across a department.

Proxies for learning

As I am wont to do, let's start with a story. In my science department we often split classes – and while it really helps from a curriculum and teaching point of view, the unintended consequence is that students are prone to comparing staff and picking favourites. Once I had a student who was convinced that her chemistry teacher was not explaining things correctly as 'she didn't get it', but her biology teacher was amazing because she found everything really easy. Naturally, I investigated by talking to the staff and looking at the books to gather evidence before meeting the student and her mother. I looked at both books. The chemistry book was poorly completed, messy, with answers written in multiple colours and doodles in the margins. The biology book was exquisite: pages of neat work all ticked off, all correct. Early indications seemed to back up the student's concerns.

But let's pause here and explore the idea of proxies. What I have just described is the use of proxies to determine the quality of explanations. Professor Robert Coe, who is, at the time of writing, director of research and evaluation at Evidence Based Education, has spent many years campaigning against poor proxies for learning. His non-exhaustive list is as follows:

1   Students are busy: lots of work is done (especially written work)

2   Students are engaged, interested, motivated

3   Students are getting attention: feedback, explanations

4   Classroom is ordered, calm, under control

5   Curriculum has been 'covered' (ie presented to students in some form)

6   (At least some) students have supplied correct answers (whether or not they really understood them or could reproduce them independently)[2]

2   R. Coe, *Improving Education: A Triumph of Hope over Experience.* Inaugural Lecture of Professor Robert Coe, Director of CEM and Professor of Education at the School of Education, Durham University, 19 June 2013, p. xii. Available at: http://www.cem.org/attachments/publications/ImprovingEducation2013.pdf.

That list is a bit depressing, isn't it? I've spent countless years trying to get my classes to fulfil that brief! I think it's worth pointing out that these things might still be useful to aspire to in the classroom. 'Poor proxies' means that having these things in place does not *guarantee* that learning will occur. They might be useful conditions if students are to be encouraged to think about the topic at hand – the one thing that does help learning – but they can be in place and students will still not think about the topic hard enough to learn it, or they will forget it later on. If learning is a change in long-term memory, then if it is not revisited it won't be learnt. Back to our story.

In discussion with the two teachers, it became clear that some of the reasons for the differences in the books were due to the level of challenge and the teachers' expectations. In chemistry, when the student was stuck, she was directed to resources that could help but given minimal guidance. This teacher's aim was to establish independence. In biology, the students could use support materials whenever they wanted; however, these materials were so helpful that answers could be copied instantly into the book with minimal thought. In both cases the difficulty was not ideal, but training helped these teachers to adjust and the performance of the class improved over time.

If we had created a quality-assurance system that focused on the quantity and neatness of books, what would have been the result? The chemistry book would have failed, and the biology book would have passed with flying colours. This is an illustration of the problems that all quality-assurance systems face: how do we know we are looking for the right thing?

Gaming the system

On top of this lies a second problem: how do we prevent gaming the system?

Social psychologist Donald Campbell has spent a large portion of his career looking at how incentivising certain metrics distorts group behaviour:

> **The more any quantitative social indicator is used for social decision-making, the more subject it will be to corruption pressures and the more apt it will be to distort and corrupt the social processes it is intended to monitor.**[3]

---

3   D. T. Campbell, Assessing the Impact of Planned Social Change, *Evaluation and Program Planning*, 2(1) (1979): 67–90 at 85.

Essentially what this means is: the more emphasis we place on a certain metric as an indicator of success, the more likely it is that the group's behaviour will change to game the system. They will devote discretionary effort to improving the metric by any means, even if it completely undermines the intended outcome.

I'll illustrate this with a simple example. Let's say one of the metrics of your quality-assurance system is to look at books and do a 'shake test': i.e. lift the book by the cover and give it a shake to see if all the worksheets and handouts are stuck in. Your rationale might be that if all the work is stuck in then it means the student has all their notes to revise from, so it's a good thing. You could also infer pride in the student's work. Unfortunately, what actually happens is that the day before the quality-assurance inspection takes place, as you walk down the corridor you see lots of students sticking loose worksheets into their books at random. A teacher who is worried about failing has stopped the lesson and devoted time to sticking in instead of learning. In another classroom, a teacher on non-contact time sits there, glue stick in hand, sticking worksheets into every book, rather than planning their lessons. Both are examples of gaming the system: the metric is being fulfilled, but the actual aim – to improve the quality of the students' education – is being undermined. In both cases the opportunity cost is high because the time it requires cannot be spent doing other things that aid learning. These are not the only ways of gaming this metric, however.

Many years ago, my mother wanted to improve her ICT skills, so she enrolled, through her local adult education centre, for a European Computer Driving License (ECDL). Its aims are outlined as follows:

The ECDL (European Computer Driving License) certification is a highly recognised qualification, it offers you a key recognition of your literacy in computer skills and is designed for novices or casual computer users and will get you to a high computer literacy standard.[4]

She really enjoyed herself and learnt valuable skills that she still uses today. In 2014 the government in Westminster decided to introduce the Progress 8 (P8) measure. Alongside this numerical metric of school performance, they overhauled the qualifications that were compliant with the performance measures. This was an attempt to prevent gaming the system, as over the previous five years students had been given a raft of coursework-heavy vocational qualifications with the aim of securing as many C or equivalent grades as possible. Unfortunately, when they culled a wide variety of less-effective vocational subjects, the ECDL was left on the list. In 2015 roughly 40,000 certificates were

4   See http://www.ecdluk.co.uk/ecdl_curriculum.html.

awarded. Fast-forward to 2017 and the number of Year 11 students sitting the ECDL qualification had risen to roughly 150,000, which is more than one quarter of all students.[5] Large consultancy groups, like PiXL,[6] were actively encouraging school leaders to enter all their cohorts for ECDL as a last-gasp measure to get them a grade that would count towards school performance metrics: gaming the system at its most pure. This is not to say that the ECDL is worthless, more that these students were not its intended audience and already possessed the skills needed to pass it. For the students involved that time would have been more valuable spent working on a subject in which they were struggling. Moving from an E to a D in another subject – say, business studies – would add more value to their personal education. However, the system encouraged schools to drag them away from that in order to improve national performance measures.

This example illustrates the effect that accountability has on decision making. The higher the stakes, the more likely it is that people will game the system. In his book *The Tyranny of Metrics*, Jerry Muller discusses many examples of this phenomenon from different professions, but the British education system is front and centre. He suggests considering the following questions if you want to reduce the chances of gaming occurring:

1   What kind of information are you thinking of measuring?

2   How useful is the information?

3   How useful are more metrics?

4   What are the costs of not relying on standardised measurement?

5   To what purpose will the measurement be put (to whom will the information be made transparent)?

6   What are the costs of acquiring the metrics?

7   Why are the people at the top of the organisation demanding performance metrics?

8   How and by whom are the performance measures developed?[7]

5   P. Nye, Some MATs Look to Have Been Hit Hard by the Withdrawal of ECDL, *FFT Education Datalab* (16 November 2018). Available at: https://ffteducationdatalab.org.uk/2018/11/some-mats-look-to-have-been-hit-hard-by-the-withdrawal-of-ecdl/.

6   J. Dickens, 'Gaming' Row Flares Up Again over Pixl Club's Advice for Schools to Use Three-Day ICT 'GCSE', *Schools Week* (22 March 2016). Available at: https://schoolsweek.co.uk/gaming-row-flares-up-again-over-pixl-clubs-advice-for-schools-to-use-three-day-ict-gcse/.

7   J. Z. Muller, *The Tyranny of Metrics* (Princeton: Princeton University Press, 2018), pp. 174–183.

Our quality-assurance system needs to keep these issues at the forefront. However we decide to carry it out, we need to remember its limitations and the reasons why we made certain choices.

Let's unpick each issue and look at how it might be applied to a school setting.

1. What kind of information are you thinking of measuring?

Humans suffer from a kind of cognitive bias called the 'availability heuristic'. Stated simply, we tend to prioritise readily available information over that which is harder to obtain. This means that the people designing the quality-assurance system will probably put more emphasis on metrics that are easy to measure and check than ones that might be more useful. In teaching, we often end up with an overemphasis on the work produced in books. It also prioritises things that can be made into a simple checklist and easily noticed.

2. How useful is the information?

Let's keep our focus on exercise books to consider this question. What does the work done in them actually tell us? Coe points to it as a poor proxy for learning, so clearly it's not all that and a bag of chips, but what can it tell us? It can tell us what is being taught, and it can give us an idea about some of the activities used in the lesson. But it doesn't tell us much about verbal questioning or other activities (e.g. the use of mini whiteboards) that have huge educational value but almost no footprint in the book. So, book scrutiny has a use but also definite limitations.

3. How useful are more metrics?

Will adding more criteria improve the information we get from the quality-assurance procedure? In general, the more metrics you have, the more inclusive and broader your judgement can be. On the other hand, more metrics might detract from your aims and increase the scope for gaming. This is one to consider if you revisit the policy in the future.

4. What are the costs of not relying on standardised measurement?

As leaders we are responsible for the education of large groups of students in our subject or pastoral teams. We have a huge moral responsibility to ensure, no matter who teaches them, that every student gets the best education we can provide. It's a weight that we will discuss in more detail in Chapter 9. There is also the added pressure that, as leaders, we are accountable for quality-assuring our teams. Standardised measurement is very easy to collate and display to line managers. It has a reassuring, although often completely fake, clarity. In short, if you find yourself under a large amount of pressure to improve student performance, standardised metrics could save your job. If you can say things like 'the number of students completing their homework increased by 25%' or 'the quality of teaching is improving in Year 7 because there was an increase of 9% in the average score for the Easter test compared to the Christmas test', you can convince people that your strategy is working. Now, you and I know that this is a very tenuous statement to make; it's essentially bordering on nonsense. However, sometimes we need this data to buy ourselves time to make the long-term changes that will actually drive up performance. Some standardised measurements may be desirable, but we need to carefully choose the most appropriate ones (and beware their limitations).

5. To what purpose will the measurement be put (to whom will the information be made transparent)?

Why is this even an issue? Surely all data should be shared? Well, if teachers don't know that we are collecting data, it can't be gamed. However, if we keep the data a secret then how can feedback be given to improve performance? It's a classic catch-22. The other extreme is to make all teachers' outcomes public by sharing them widely. This public name-and-shame strategy has obvious drawbacks in terms of motivation and group morale. We will need to carefully consider what metrics we share and which we keep confidential.

6. What are the costs of acquiring the metrics?

This one is fascinating from an educational perspective. In the corporate world the cost is a very real cash value associated with the creation of a system and paying the wages of those responsible for running it. In schools the biggest resource is time. Every decision has an opportunity cost as it results in something else not being done. The opportunity cost for book scrutiny is probably low. It will be a few hours of a leader's time every quality-assurance cycle. On the other hand, if we were to embrace a more holistic quality-assurance model of visiting 25% of lessons taught in our department then the opportunity cost would be huge. When considering question 6, we can now see the value of looking at books. Question 6 often overrides a lot of the other rules in school systems. We will have to fight the urge to follow the quickest route and instead tread the more effective but time-consuming one.

7. Why are the people at the top of the organisation demanding performance metrics?

I once worked with a colleague who hated performance metrics, which she referred to as 'bullshit spreadsheets'. There will have been times in your career when I'm sure you have felt similarly – I know I have. School leaders have generated and analysed ever-more teaching and assessment data over the last decade or so. The proliferation of ICT and the desire for evidence to support self-evaluation has created a cottage industry within schools and by external consultants and multi-academy trusts. Essentially, what it boils down to is the simple fact that, as leaders, we cannot see every lesson. We need to find a way to judge the general quality of our product – education in our subject – by sampling a series of metrics. Our line managers in turn are even further removed. They are responsible for the performance of our department even though they often have no subject-specific experience or expertise. While as subject leaders we can go into a class and gauge the quality using our prior knowledge, a non-specialist cannot. The production of metrics becomes even more valuable and the proxies become proof. Our system needs to be able to communicate this contradiction to both line managers and team members. It needs to recognise this dual purpose to avoid being pulled off course by senior leadership's need for proof. (We will discuss how to manage up and ensure your line managers are on board with your decisions in Chapter 8.)

8. How and by whom are the measures of performance developed?

Often the answer to this is 'By the senior leadership team in a meeting and behind closed doors.' This may sound cynical but given the fast-moving, time-poor nature of school leadership roles it is often the case that decisions are made in a vacuum. Often leaders will prioritise ease of measurement when designing a metric. This is how we end up with things like our 'shake test'. The next step is a series of assumptions that links the proxy (the exercise book is the lesson) to the metric (worksheets are stuck in) to the conclusion (the teacher is organised and so the lessons must be good). These decisions are often made in conjunction with senior leaders who may no longer understand a classroom teacher's day-to-day work. Egocentric bias affects all of us. In leadership it manifests in thinking that our decisions will have no negative effects on classroom teachers, because we would have coped fine. I also like to call this the 'it just takes five minutes' rule. If your justification for a new policy has ever been 'it will only take the teacher five extra minutes', then you might have fallen foul of this inescapable bias too. Those five minutes quickly get compounded by all the other five-minute tasks and the result is a huge amount of time. To avoid this we will need to try to develop our own metrics, some of which should be developed in collaboration with team members. This way we can receive feedback from those who will be most affected and understand the implications behind the decisions we make.

> **Egocentric bias:** A cognitive bias whereby you remember your past performance as being much better than it actually was.

Creating your quality-assurance process

Your quality-assurance process needs to efficiently determine the quality of education provided by your team. This is an important leadership role, so it is worth devoting time to. When considering our eight questions and the pragmatic issues of day-to-day departmental leadership responsibilities, a mixed approach that uses lesson visits and book scrutiny might be the best option. To improve efficiency, we should also make use of line managers, guiding them closely to focus on specific things that are easy to judge and record.

You will need to make your own decisions about your quality-assurance process based on your context. Things that might affect your decision will include, but not be limited to:

- The whole-school quality-assurance policy. Are there any non-negotiables?
- The amount of leadership time you have within your department.
- The confidence level you have in your team leaders' ability to determine the quality of teaching across the department.
- Your preferred ratio of lesson visits to book scrutinies.
- What you deem that it is possible to determine from book scrutiny.
- Whether you need to measure quality or develop staff collaboratively.

The final point is a crucial one. At different times in your career, you will need to adjust your approach. If you are leading a department which has struggled with performance recently, there might be a pressure to develop metrics to determine the level of consistency and ensure that key strategies are being used correctly. This will require a quality-assurance system that allows trends to be seen over time. It will also favour more direct, tick-or-cross feedback over a coaching model (more on which in Chapter 8). This is question 6 in action. These metrics can be used to allay the fears of senior leaders and demonstrate the positive direction in which you are leading the team. In contrast, a highly successful department might be focused on taking the time to develop their staff in more flexible ways, as the basics are already in place. They have the confidence of their line management, so their metrics will be different.

Next, I'm going to outline the rationale behind my quality-assurance system. Consider this a worked example, but do not think that I am saying it is perfect or the only model; schools are so different, and each team has its own nuances and eccentricities to be considered. My hope is that this will give you some pointers that you might find useful and maybe challenge some preconceived notions about how to measure the quality of teaching.

Work scrutiny

My system uses book-looks. I can't avoid the fact that books are readily available and a consistent feature in all lessons. However, I need to anticipate the potential negative consequences of using work scrutiny, so my book-look policy will be based on the following principles:

1   Books are a poor proxy for learning.

2   Book-looks are needed because leaders cannot visit all lessons.

3   Books can tell us about routines, effort and standards.

4   Books can help us to see the range and scope of the curriculum being enacted in the classroom.

5   Teachers who are not maintaining desired standards are not falling short on purpose or being lazy.

6   All staff can benefit from sharing practice and discussing students' work.

I think we've already covered principles 1–3 sufficiently. As far as principle 4 goes, books do give us valuable indications of the range and depth of teaching that students are experiencing in the curriculum we designed. If we reflect on our vision for the curriculum, books might be able to help us see whether this is being realised in the classroom. We can also determine if certain teaching and learning principles – which we discussed in Chapter 2 – are being embedded effectively. What follows are the questions I ask myself when looking at books.

Before the books are opened:

- What does excellence look like in this subject? What do I expect to see/what should we see in the books?

- Are classes of similar abilities progressing through the curriculum at a similar rate?

While looking at books:

- Is the level of work being asked of the students appropriately ambitious?

- Why is this being taught now? What did the lesson build on? What do the books show about lesson sequencing?

- How am I certain that the curriculum is being enacted/followed consistently by all teachers (including non-specialists)? What do these books tell me about the implementation of the curriculum?

- Do the books show evidence of our teaching and learning principles in action? For example, do they show regular retrieval practice or opportunities for extended writing 'power hours'?

- Do these books show evidence of explicit literacy teaching – for example, the introduction of key words and the correction of spelling, punctuation and grammar?

- Is there evidence of students acting on feedback (including spelling, punctuation and grammar, where this is expected)?

- Why is this topic important both in the grand scheme of things and in preparation for assessment? How does it relate to what students need to learn (powerful knowledge)?

- Is the work optimised for students to spend their time thinking about the content?

- What is the level of demand on the students?

- Are students succeeding at challenging tasks or making useful mistakes that will lead to success?

- What do exercise books indicate about the curriculum that is being taught in lessons?

- Are the principles of concrete to abstract, simple to complex, components to composites, and interleaving being used effectively?

Principle 5 is worth stating explicitly while performing the book-look to prevent leaders falling into a fundamental attribution error: thinking that poor results are due to personal character flaws instead of circumstances. It reduces the stakes and focuses the process on staff development. Principle 6 is also key. It reminds us that all teachers need to improve, and that we often have much to learn from each other. It also prevents leaders from putting themselves on a pedestal. We will not have all the solutions and often classroom teachers have innovative, useful strategies that we can spread through our department.

As far as work scrutiny goes, what follows is the procedure I settled on. Hopefully, you'll find this a helpful starting point:

- We will devote a portion of every department meeting to looking at the books of a particular year group. If it's a useful thing to do then we should find the time to do it properly.

- We will bring in a sample from each class and discuss the quality of the work in trios. Trios take the formality away but give everyone a chance to get into a meaningful discussion.

- We will feed back good practice and write down next steps. During the discussion, we will focus on the positive and generate momentum. Keep the issues low-key to avoid embarrassing staff.

- These next steps will be collated by the head of department to follow up issues and check for department-wide training needs.

- Any members of staff who are not compliant with the feedback policy will be met at a later date and support will be provided.

Lesson visits

The second part of the quality-assurance system involves lesson visits. We can't see every lesson, of course, but we can try to devote as much time as possible to visiting a variety of lessons to provide an insight into day-to-day teaching. Often the learning walk policy contains a myriad of tick boxes and lists. While there will be certain non-negotiables in the school teaching and learning policy, it is vital that we remember our list of metric mistakes and try to create space for contextual comments and nuance. We use Rosenshine's Principles of Instruction (as we discussed in Chapter 2) to provide broad categories of lesson structure. This means that when I walk into a lesson, I can get a feel for what category the current activity fits into from a list of four options:

1   Retrieval.

2   Explanation and modelling.

3   Questioning.

4   Student practice.

I am not expecting every lesson to include all four, but while I am observing the lesson I can record my thoughts on these key aspects. We also have an 'other' box on our pro-forma in case the lesson does not cover any of these areas, which is rare, or if we see another issue that needs addressing. This could be about behaviour management, for example. I'm sure there are a multitude of ways to gather the feedback: the important thing is that whatever method you use allows for a useful conversation to happen later and avoids the pressure of fulfilling metrics for the sake of it. Here is an example of the template we use:

Learning walk record sheet			
Teacher		Observer	
Class		Subject	
Date		Lesson	

Simple non-negotiables (tick or cross in the box)	
Do the students enter the class in accordance with whole-school policy? (E.g. do-now activity, silent start, etc.)	
Does the teacher use the whole-school behaviour policy to ensure disruption-free learning?	
Is homework set in accordance with department policy?	
Is the class following the curriculum? (E.g. progressing through schemes of work, teacher setting appropriate challenge in tasks, etc.)	

Retrieval:	Explanation and modelling:

Questioning:	Practice:

Other comments:

Single improvement target:

Figure 7: An example learning walk record sheet

Tackling the capacity problem

Sustainable improvement through incremental coaching is often the aim of a lot of learning walk policies. But actually getting this to work is incredibly difficult. It takes time and doesn't fit easily within the six-week time frame that is often used. So how do we build capacity into an already busy day with many competing priorities? Well, put simply, it must be a priority. It needs time. I honestly think that the choices a middle leader must make when it comes to prioritising their time are incredibly difficult. But consider this: if the only thing you do is increase your team's teaching ability by 10%, what will happen? My guess is that the students will be grateful and perform well, results will improve, and senior leaders will be happy. If you are spending more time doing operational tasks than developing your teachers, yes, you will meet every deadline and your department will run smoothly but you will be letting your students down. This is not to say that these things aren't important for departmental performance; it's just that they are much less important than what goes on in classrooms day in and day out. To avoid the very real drag towards admin and crisis management, I have found it best to diarise time for learning walks.

My senior leadership team (SLT) link is expected to do learning walks to quality-assure teaching. While he is exceptional in many ways, he is not a subject specialist. This means asking him to give advice on the science-specific aspects of teaching is relatively pointless. But, fortunately, teaching features a large domain of generic skills that he can help monitor and improve. Routines and generic classroom practice are areas that all leaders can support. Most teachers have room for improvement in certain aspect of routines or classroom practice. If the school has a shared teaching language, senior leaders can support staff in developing effective classroom habits that align with the school's ethos and policies. They can determine if routines are well established and effective. They can observe the techniques used to gain students' attention, questioning strategies, and application of the behaviour policy. These are all valuable things that help provide a snapshot of conditions for learning. In Chapter 2 we discussed how routines are the bedrock of good teaching, so by moving senior leaders into the role of supporting routines, they are providing a valuable source of feedback and quality assurance. A further advantage is that these visits – so-called drop-ins – need only be ten minutes long, so allow a large sample to be taken, as SLT can visit numerous classes in an hour window. Figure 8 is an example of a drop-in proforma, with the first section completed as a worked example, but your approach will vary depending on the metrics you prioritise.

Start of lesson:	Was it seen?	Comments
Threshold	Y	Teacher was on door and welcoming students in.
Warm-strict greetings	Y	Particularly liked the way you challenged Steven's uniform.
Regular retrieval practice	Y	Six questions as a do-now activity.
Routines regarding folders and resource distribution	Y	Smooth orderly entrance. Students knew what to do and class settled quickly.
During lesson (at all times):	Was it seen?	Comments
Appropriate method of gaining silence (signal, pause, insist)		
Use of warnings in a warm-strict way		
Lowest possible sanction (to prevent disruption to learning)		

During explanations:	Was it seen?	Comments
Clarity/volume of voice		
Concise effective instructions (brighten the lines)		
Time limits		
During questioning:	Was it seen?	Comments
Cold call		
No opt out		
Right is right		
Say it in a sentence		
During independent practice:	Was it seen?	Comments
Tracking not watching		
High levels of purposeful circulation		
Calm productive climate		
Narrating positive behaviour		
End of lesson:	Was it seen?	Comments
Orderly dismissal		
Rewards issued		
Any other comments:		

Figure 8: An example science SLT walk-through proforma

When we put all these principles together, this is what emerges as my commitment to staff:

- I am going to devote two hours a week of my leadership time to learning walks.

- I am going to direct my fellow department leaders to devote one hour a fortnight to learning walks.

- Every meeting I have with a leader will be no more than 30 minutes long, and the second half will be a paired learning walk.

- I will ask my SLT line manager to do drop-in visits to check that staff are using *Teach Like a Champion 2.0* techniques and our behaviour policy correctly, identifying any reluctant learners.

- Every learning walk will include a face-to-face follow-up discussion with the member of staff, and only one target will be identified. If they are part-time then mutually consented email might be required.

- We will keep a shared log so that I can see at a glance if issues are arising. If there are global issues, or problems due to department or whole-school systems, these will be addressed in our CPD time.

- Staff will be visited by the same leader over the course of a term. This aims to create a collegiate approach and make it easier to improve the one specific target over the term.

- I will operate an open-door policy and will welcome staff to watch me teach at any time. One team leader will be directed to take a learning walk through my classes on top of this. No one is above the group.

Overall, this quality-assurance system tries to find a balance between the need to measure and the need to develop practice collaboratively and in a low-stakes environment. Figure 9 (see page 88) shows the various tiers and how they relate to each other.

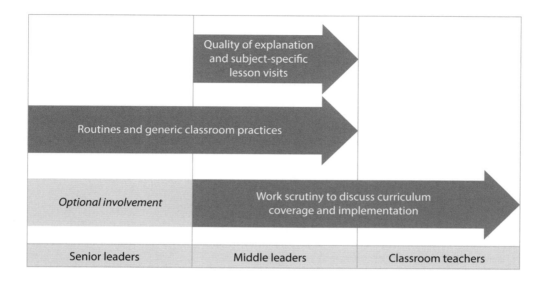

Figure 9: The various levels of engagement with the quality-assurance system

Recap

- Quality assurance is a vital aspect of middle leadership in schools.

- Often the most convenient metrics to measure will not give us a clear picture of the quality of teaching.

- Improvement in a metric does not indicate improvement in teacher performance, unless the metrics are carefully balanced.

- Raising stakes is more likely to encourage gaming of the system instead of permanent improvements in teacher proficiency.

- Work scrutiny is a useful tool, but it is a poor proxy for learning so needs to be used cautiously.

- Lesson visits can give us a tool to identify areas of improvement for all teachers.

- By maintaining the observer–observed pair we can build a coaching-style relationship to support development.

- Non-subject-specialist members of the SLT can focus on generic routines and teaching practices providing capacity for leaders and a valuable feedback opportunity for staff.

Reflect

- What metrics do I need to monitor closely?

- What metrics does my line manager value, and do I agree?

- How will I ensure that there is little gaming of the system?

- Am I sure that I am choosing metrics based on their value, not their ease of measurement?

- What balance of book scrutiny and lesson visits will work for my team?

- Are my SLT comfortable looking at certain metrics as non-subject-specialists? Is there a training need here?

Chapter 5

Leading teacher development

> Every teacher needs to improve, not because they are not good enough, but because they can be even better.
>
> **Dylan Wiliam**[1]

There is no such thing as the perfect teacher: we can all improve. We will be aware of some of our strengths and weaknesses, and others will be hiding in our blind spots (more on this in Chapter 6). Staff are by far the most important resource in a school. Schools, rightly, invest a large portion of their time and resources in developing teachers. It is a key middle leadership role to model strong teaching practices and to support others to reach their potential. In this chapter we will discuss the ways in which we can create a climate of continuous improvement within our team, leverage the idea of desirable difficulties to ensure efficiency of improvement, and organise tiers of CPD.

At the same time, middle leaders are expected to carry out a multitude of other tasks during the day. Their capacity to devote time to planning their own lessons and developing their own classroom practice is greatly diminished. This was acutely brought to my attention the day I accepted my head of department role. The head of PE came up to me and proclaimed, 'Congratulations! You'll never teach a great lesson again!' This was somewhat tongue-in-cheek, but it demonstrates a hidden truth that few will admit: when you are a middle leader, you have to monitor the quality of teaching, develop teachers and somehow try to live up to your own standards! I put this unspoken truth right up there with 'babies are boring for the first six months' and 'not all opinions are equal'. It is not just the loss of time available to plan your own lessons, but the amount of thinking time lost to considering the larger areas of responsibility beyond your own lessons.

---

1   D. Wiliam, Dylan Wiliam: Teaching Not a Research-Based Profession, *TES* (30 May 2019). Available at: https://www.tes.com/news/dylan-wiliam-teaching-not-research-based-profession.

Why don't we just get rid of all the weak teachers?

I am sure you have your own opinions about the teachers in your school: there will likely be those who are generally agreed to be good and those who are seen as the weak links. As leaders, our job is to secure the best possible teaching for our students, so the simple solution must be to just get rid of the weak teachers and hire some better ones, right?

When you pose this question to some leaders, their first response is 'I would love to, but I wouldn't be able to hire enough teachers to replace them!' This response is a classic case of misguided certainty in measurement. Recruitment issues aside, the truth is that it is incredibly hard to evaluate teacher performance. Take the story of Tim Clifford from *Weapons of Math Destruction* by Cathy O'Neil.[2] Tim, a middle school English teacher for 25 years, received a score of 6 out of 100 in the New York standardised teacher rankings. He was shocked but, due to a lack of feedback, taught in exactly the same way the following year. He was even more shocked when at the end of that year he received a rating of 96 out of 100! While this anecdote is not conclusive evidence, it does go some way to illustrate the volatility of teacher evaluations for the simple fact that student outcomes are the result of so many variables. Speaking personally, there have been times in my career when I have had very positive evaluations and others when I have been, to put it mildly, disappointed. In both cases I think I was essentially the same teacher, although I am willing to admit that I might not be the most impartial judge.

The evidence suggests that most teachers improve during their first five years and then plateau.[3] The reason for this – as with so many other issues in schools – is complicated. The school environment has been found to play a large role. As leaders we can work to establish conditions within our area of responsibility that will help our colleagues flourish.

---

2   C. O'Neil, *Weapons of Math Destruction: How Big Data Increases Inequality and Threatens Democracy* (New York: Penguin Random House, 2016).

3   M. A. Kraft and J. P. Papay, Can Professional Environments in Schools Promote Teacher Development? Explaining Heterogeneity in Returns to Teaching Experience, *Educational Effectiveness and Policy Analysis*, 36(4) (2014): 476–500.

How do schools often go about improving teaching and why doesn't it work?

In my experience, the most common way in which schools go about improving teaching is to publish a set of agreed criteria for 'good' teaching and then quality-assure their staff against the criteria. Staff who are found not to be meeting these expectations are then given increasing levels of formal support. These support packages start with meeting the head of department once a week. They then go through a series of steps over a few terms and end up with formal capability proceedings and the threat of termination of contract. This ensures that all staff meet a minimum expectation. This obviously works, and now all teachers are good and everything is awesome. Or not.

This approach has several drawbacks:

1   It creates a stigma whereby support and development is seen as being offered due to apparent failure.

2   Staff that just about meet the criteria are not supported as much as they might need to be.

3   Strong teachers get completely ignored.

Most importantly, any high-stakes criteria can lead to gaming the system (as we saw in Chapter 4). I'm sure we have all fallen foul of this (*cough* triple marking *cough*). I once was so worried about a book-look that I came in on a Sunday and wrote extra comments in the margins in the gap between students' first and second drafts. This was the feedback I had given verbally, but I knew that if it wasn't written down, I would fail. A good rule of thumb is: if it doesn't help the students, it's a waste of time.

What about the teachers who are identified as needing support?

The formal support packages commonly used in schools create a high-stakes, short-term, intense environment with two or three large areas of focus. If the issue is with the teacher's skills in the classroom, then the degree of difficulty in the targets is probably too high for the support package to be effective. Imagine that you are this teacher – maybe you have even been there yourself? They are losing planning time to attend support meetings, are demoralised by a huge feeling of failure and are under a huge amount of pressure to hit multiple targets in just a few weeks.[4]

What about the rest of us?

To solve drawbacks 2 and 3, schools often have a rolling CPD program. Normally this is a mix of voluntary and compulsory sessions, and will probably include INSET days, learning communities and peer-to-peer coaching. This too definitely works, so all staff should improve, right? Well, obviously not, as any teacher who has been to a whole-day CPD event can attest. You might gain one or two nuggets to take back to the classroom, but large-scale change is rare.

Two factors that we know are hugely important for students' learning are often ignored in teacher development:

1   The value of deliberate practice to develop mastery.

2   The power of desirable difficulties.

Chapter 2 discussed the power of deliberate practice for the student. The most frustrating thing for me is that while we know all these things about learning, when it comes to teacher CPD we completely ignore them! Teachers' brains are no different to students', so when designing our CPD programme we should be able to embed some of these principles into our sessions. The main implication is that teachers need time to practise a particular technique or skill so that they can embed it in their classroom teaching. Experienced teachers are not novices, so they will probably need less time than a student will to develop mastery, but in areas of weakness they might need to devote a substantial amount of time in order for it to become a usable technique. This means that we cannot do CPD on everything: we will have to prioritise. Better to master five things than cover 25 but master nothing. You see, it is just like teaching students!

Get Better Faster by Paul Bambrick–Santoyo is an excellent training guide for developing teachers.[5] Its stroke of genius is that it prioritises visible aspects of teaching practice in order of importance. For example, it prioritises classroom routines above leading a discussion. The logic being that if you haven't got strong routines, you won't be able to leverage maximum learning from a discussion. Whatever your list contains, accepting that some things are

---

4   I have been this teacher. I have had times in my career when I have been considered an excellent teacher and other times when I was considered weak. In both instances, I don't think I was that different in my teaching, but the criteria I was judged against was the key variable. The things that did improve my teaching: CogSciSci (https://cogscisci.wordpress.com/), researchED (https://researched.org.uk/) and Twitter.

5   P. Bambrick-Santoyo, *Get Better Faster: A 90-Day Plan for Coaching New Teachers* (San Francisco, CA: Jossey-Bass, 2016).

higher priority than others is incredibly important. This allows you to carefully choose what training to offer. You will have to make difficult decisions when choosing what to prioritise. As a rule of thumb, my preference is to start with routines and follow up with questioning. Once all staff have these two aspects of practice in place, then you can diversify.

What are desirable difficulties?

Robert Bjork first coined the term 'desirable difficulties' in 1994 to describe the 'Goldilocks zone' of optimum learning.[6] Tasks should be hard enough to be effective but easy enough to motivate learners to try. Put simply, we often make our decisions by the rule: is the juice worth the squeeze? As teachers we spend a lot of our time considering the level of desirable difficulty in our learning activities, but as leaders I wonder how often we consider this in our teacher improvement strategies?

Desirable difficulties in teacher development

For most teachers, the best way to deliver improvement is to work on small areas of practice incrementally. Teachers agree on an area to develop via discussion with the observer, coach or mentor. They devote deliberate practice to it at the end of the feedback conversation and in their lessons over time. Changes don't become habits overnight: staff need time to build new techniques into their current mental model of teaching, so they become a permanent aspect of their practice. To support the teacher, the same observer visits further lessons to provide guidance on their progress. Only once this area has been developed will they agree upon the next target. In this way, every teacher has one priority that they are working on, but only one. In my opinion this approach is akin to diffusion (or an ion engine if you prefer your models to have a physics slant). If we can maintain a small improvement gradient over a longer timescale, we can keep all teachers developing in a sustainable way. No single teacher gets 100% of our attention and improvement is part of the everyday culture. On any given day, the improvements feel small, but over a year they aggregate into permanent positive change. This is desirable difficulties and deliberate practice in action.

To illustrate, consider Figure 10. Teacher A lacks proficiency at this point in time. They cannot be left to plateau here: training must be challenging enough to move them along

---

6   In National Research Council, *Learning, Remembering, Believing: Enhancing Human Performance*, eds D. Druckman and R. Bjork (Washington, DC: The National Academies Press, 1994).

the proficiency continuum. They can't jump straight to high proficiency either.[7] There will be broad structural issues with their teaching or planning that will need to be prioritised. By picking the most important aspect and making it a focus they can develop in a sustainable way. Conversely, teacher B is a highly proficient teacher. They might routinely get incredibly positive feedback; however, it is our duty to find out what their next step is. It will probably be minute and technical. The aim is still to provide them with the opportunity to develop, as – as Dylan Wiliam tells us – we can always improve. By helping them to do so, we show that we care about their contribution to the team – and we exemplify that in our department no one is above improvement (even though our depiction of the gradient has an end point, there is no real limit to improvement in practice).

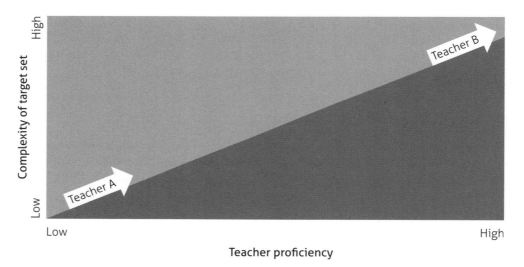

Figure 10: The teaching proficiency improvement gradient

How to deliver the feedback, and the types of conversations that will help teachers A and B develop, will be covered in more detail in Chapter 8. A quick note on the improvement gradient, as I have heard people talking about 'stepping up' their teaching. I deliberately imagine the improvement gradient as a slope for a few reasons. Firstly, gradients are slopes. Secondly, and more importantly, I wanted to have a model that implied that if you don't seek to refine your teaching, you can easily slide back down. When things happen and life takes our focus off our teaching, it is perfectly understandable that we are less

---

7   One caveat: if it is not an issue of skill, but rather one of motivation, they might be able to jump straight to proficient. That will necessitate a very different conversation and a more formal process, possibly with the involvement of human resources.

proficient. These things happen. It is vital that, as leaders, we realise that even our best teachers can slide back and might need more intensive support at certain times.

Creating a culture of continuous improvement

Creating a culture of continuous improvement requires all staff to participate. Often our best teachers are keen to get better and motivated to take part, seeking feedback and inviting visitors into their classrooms. Our weakest need to improve, so are mandated to participate and receive close monitoring. However, our average teachers will not fit into either category and can easily be ignored as they drift along.

If we can establish a culture that makes all staff active participants in their own improvement, it provides a number of benefits. Firstly, it ensures that all staff receive appreciation and feedback. Secondly, it encourages day-to-day discussions about teaching and classroom issues, creating informal development discussions. Finally, and most importantly, it reduces the possible negative consequences of imposing formal staged support for weaker teachers. From an outside perspective they are just being supported like everyone else. To the head of department they are top priority, they get more frequent learning walks, more frank conversations and less choice of next steps. There will still be accountability and they know that improvement needs to come, but it will come without the loss of morale and will ensure permanent change.

How to structure CPD

Once we have established a climate of continuous improvement, we can focus on the best ways to deliver CPD. There are many different ways to structure CPD, so I'm going to discuss how I think it works best. I want to create the structure for a CPD system that allows for incremental improvement and is flexible to suit a range of needs. In Chapter 4 we recognised the value of learning walks for development. We also discussed how having the same person conduct these walks over a term allows the relationship to build and collaboration to occur. Therefore, learning walks will be a key tool in our strategy; indeed, they are the foundation of my CPD approach. Learning walk feedback is one of the sources of information that helps me to decide what to prioritise. Senior and middle leaders will need to be aware of this and a system will need to be created to ensure that these records are easy to locate and digest.

I can't just be reactionary. I need to ensure that we have a shared vision for what we want our students to experience in their lessons. By spending time thinking about how I want our department to look and feel from a student's perspective I can start to create an end goal. Next, this can be broken down into a road map – from the current situation towards our ideal (which might be very far away at the moment) – and we can prioritise the steps to take first. This ties in with the ideas discussed in Chapter 2. Once the road map is in place, I can see clearly what our initial focus for CPD should be. If this is taking place in the summer, then we can plan for our first training days in September and begin to instil these new ideas from the first day of the new school year.

I now have our priorities in order and a way to monitor and adjust them as the year progresses. Brilliant! 10 points to Gryffindor! Unfortunately, that is the easy part. The hard part is creating a system to encourage teachers, who are incredibly busy, to partake in regular deliberate practice. This is where you will start to run into the limitations of your context. In reality, it is incredibly hard to get what you want when you are not the person in charge of the school calendar. As a middle leader there are things you can do to manage up the chain of command, but we must also be realistic.

What follows is a summary of the conditions we need in place in order to get buy-in from staff and thus achieve our aims. Whatever your context or levels of influence, if you do your best to get these into your system, you will be able to make the most of your CPD time. So, you will need:

● Agreement that staff will only focus on one area at a time.

● An element of choice. It won't be a completely free choice, but it should aim to focus all staff on picking from a range of strategies that we know work well. The most competent staff can have more freedom; others may be directed to high-priority areas.

● Time for staff to discuss and adapt principles.

● Opportunities for subjects to be together to discuss subject-specific issues. For example, a performing arts department might consist of music and drama teachers, but they will value time to discuss these contexts separately on occasion.

If you can find a way to get these ideals established, then you can be confident that you are doing your best to develop your staff.

What does the evidence say?

Mary Kennedy's 2019 review of CPD approaches tells us what features will support teacher development.[8] It clearly shows a strong link between effective CPD and programmes which try to avoid overly prescriptive standardised techniques. She identifies the following components of good CPD systems:

- Programmes which help develop insights into how techniques can be applied to a teacher's context.

- Using experienced teachers to share their insights and ideas around an issue and demonstrate a principle's flexibility.

- A focus on the idea that all staff can improve.

- Commitment to cover why a technique is used, when it should be used and how it can change in different scenarios.

- An appreciation for the energy expenditure in changing practice and breaking habits.

Figure 11 (see page 100) is an outline of my preference for CPD structure. It has four tiers to it of increasing specificity and flexibility. The aim is to find a way to fit all our desirables into the time available in a sustainable way. I have arranged the tiers into a pyramid. Generally educators love a pyramid. In this case the width demonstrates my thoughts on the relative importance to overall success.

Tier 1 is the foundation: the learning walk cycle. This provides two main things. Firstly, the initial observations of areas of strength and weakness. Secondly, it also gives an opportunity for instructional coaching or mentoring conversations and builds those candid, trusting relationships between middle leaders and team members.

Tier 2 is whole-school CPD sessions that run across several INSET days. These tend to focus on whole-school objectives like behaviour management, routines, questioning, etc. The required techniques are modelled, and examples and relevant non-examples are shown. Within these sessions there is always time for staff to discuss the strategy and explore how it fits into what they currently do in the classroom. Importantly, these discussions are curated so that teachers from a broad range of subjects are put in groups, so the applicability conditions can be discussed by comparing implementation across a range of subjects. Cue questions are provided to lead the discussion in an effective direction. If

---

8   M. M. Kennedy, How We Learn About Teacher Learning, *Review of Research in Education*, 43(1) (2019): 138–162. Available at: https://journals.sagepub.com/doi/pdf/10.3102/0091732X19838970.

unstructured, the conversations will quickly dissolve into chit-chat or, worse, some teachers dominating the time with a particular viewpoint or opinion. These sessions finish with time to practise the strategy. This can involve role play (cringe, I know, but it is effective) or discussion of a series of scenarios. Sometimes it involves planning a lesson which incorporates the strategy. This final discussion can be completed in departments and allows them to share ideas that have been gleaned from other departments during their initial conversations.

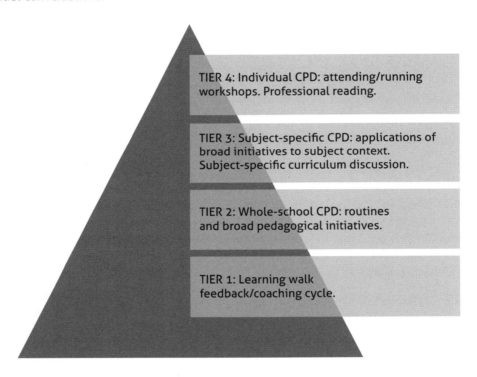

TIER 4: Individual CPD: attending/running workshops. Professional reading.

TIER 3: Subject-specific CPD: applications of broad initiatives to subject context. Subject-specific curriculum discussion.

TIER 2: Whole-school CPD: routines and broad pedagogical initiatives.

TIER 1: Learning walk feedback/coaching cycle.

Figure 11: The four tiers of CPD

Tier 3 is subject-specific CPD. First introduced to me by Shaun Allison, we protect meeting time once a fortnight and allocate this to departments.[9] These subject CPD sessions are time for the department to meet and discuss the topics being taught in the next fortnight. Explanations, misconceptions and relevant reading materials can all be discussed and debated. Often this is tied into the CPD training needs that learning walks

9   S. Allison, Subject Planning and Development Sessions, *Class Teaching* [blog] (19 September 2016). Available at: https://classteaching.wordpress.com/2016/09/19/subject-planning-and-development-sessions/.

have identified – for example, we might discuss strategies to improve 'wait time'[10] while discussing the best questions to ask after demonstrating the electric motor in science. Middle leaders run these sessions with high levels of autonomy. Senior leaders are sent the minutes so that they are aware of what occurred and of any next steps that might need their support.

The final tier is the flexible CPD option. We award a disaggregated INSET day, and the staff are expected to engage in CPD in a way that suits them. They could be attending twilight CPD sessions based on areas identified as their targets during learning walks. These sessions are relatively informal and run by staff who show expertise in a particular area. They focus on staff discussing the strengths and limitations of specific approaches and reflecting on how they would apply them in their classroom and subject. This is not always the best solution for some staff, so we also credit professional reading and attendance at conferences outside of school hours. This way we are acknowledging the work that some of our more engaged staff do on their own initiative because we know that this will be catalysing their development. Staff are asked to complete a simple log to demonstrate what they have done and what they have taken away from it. It is up to middle leaders to check this and ensure its quality.

Let's use an example to pull all these threads together and see what this feels like to an average teacher. Let's call him Adam and let's say he teaches science.[11] Adam starts the year in September with INSET that includes training on behaviour management and school routines. This includes specific guidance on how to apply the school behaviour policy, routines for the starts and ends of lessons and the whole-school aim to improve questioning. As term starts, he gets seen once a fortnight by a middle leader on a learning walk. A senior leader also drops in on him for a quick snapshot on routines. The feedback cycle gives him the target to improve his use of wait time. This is now his focus. In subject-specific CPD, the department discusses examiners' reports from last year's GCSE exams and what they tell us about possible deficits in students' abilities. Several actions are agreed, and the department separates into specialisms to co-plan how they could improve their teaching. As half-term approaches, he receives feedback that his use of wait time is now excellent.

He agrees a new target to work on to do with using storytelling structures in his explanations. Before Christmas he is asked to co-deliver a CPD session in January as part of the CPD carousel. Having gained confidence from a subject-specific CPD session on balancing equations, he is confident that he can provide advice and explain the benefits he has

10 Wait time is a *Teach Like a Champion 2.0* technique. It is the idea that after asking a question to the class you wait for an extended period of time so that students can think of their answer. It is incredibly simple, but also very hard to stick to in the time-pressured world of the classroom.
11 And my mother says I lack imagination!

found with this approach. By the time January comes around, he has made tangible progress in his teaching. The spring term provides him with six learning walks, some of which include his line manager so that he can receive specific feedback on a planned activity, and 12 drop-ins. He has had subject-specific training six times and learnt new ways of explaining electrical circuits and evolution – two areas he found difficult before. He co-delivers one CPD session, attends another on literacy where he discusses with English teachers and the special educational needs coordinator (SENCO) how best to embed literacy into his lessons, and uses his remaining three hours to read blogs on narratives and learning. The last day of the spring term is a disaggregated INSET day in lieu of the time spent on professional development. The summer term contains no optional CPD sessions, but the rest of the programme continues. While he is generally receiving positive feedback from his SLT drop-ins over the year, he has had some trouble applying the behaviour policy effectively with a Year 10 low-ability group. Through drop-ins he has been working on using the least invasive approach and his SLT link has diarised to drop in on this class to offer advice and adjustments. Over the year this has improved.

A word on inquiry work

I know of lots of schools that prefer their CPD to be based around staff pursuing an inquiry question. Historically, I have been part of inquiry CPD groups and have even ran them. However, I haven't put them into my CPD model. The main reason for this is because I think that they don't work for most staff. Unless the teacher has a particular passion for an area of research – making them pick a topic, look at the evidence and experiment with approaches before reviewing the outcomes – it is something for which they don't have the time or inclination. Instead, I want to provide spaces for professional discussions and make sure that CPD leaders foster reflective processes within our sessions. I hope that these approaches will provide some of the benefits of inquiry work – the solution-focused, low-stakes environment, etc. – without the laborious processes. I'm sure that when done well, it works well; I just think that it is hard to do it well in the time available. If you want to have it as part of your CPD process, it's best included as an option to fill the six hours of flexible time, possibly for recently qualified teachers.

There are lots of CPD models that can work given the right circumstances. You will need to be pragmatic and fit your goals into the whole-school system. The important thing is that you create a culture that allows your team to have:

- Agency in their teaching practice.
- Professional discussion of different solutions.

- Respectful challenge of each other's opinions when necessary.
- A structure that is based on research, but in a highly accessible way.
- Recognition of their strengths and expertise and those of the team.

Recap

- All teachers can improve, so our teacher development strategy should be inclusive.
- Removing the stigma and lowering the stakes of supporting weaker teachers will encourage them to improve, and continue to improve, without gaming the system.
- Prioritising your list of desired improvements allows for effective incremental change.
- CPD is a vital aspect of any teacher development programme.
- However, teacher development is more than CPD. It is the bread and butter of middle leadership. It should be prioritised above operational tasks.
- Learning walks and feedback provide a vital avenue for teacher development and data gathering.
- Desirable difficulties and the model of working memory should be considered when designing optimal teacher development processes.
- At the surface, all teachers should seem to have a similar experience, but underneath those who need more direct support and a faster timeline require assertive mentoring.
- To create staff agency and buy-in, CPD should be tiered and flexible.
- Recognising the work that staff put into their own professional development fosters a culture that values improvement and commitment.

Reflect

- How can I create a climate of continuous improvement?
- Does my current CPD model provide the flexibility to support all staff to improve?
- How do staff in need of more formal support receive it without reducing their morale significantly?

- Do I spend enough time developing teaching? If not, how can I ensure that I protect development time?

- Who in my department has a particular strength that should be shared widely?

- Do I have access to the best evidence-informed solutions? Who in my school can support with this?

Chapter 6
Decision making

> I believe in two principles: Your attitude is more important than your capabilities.
> Similarly, your decision is more important than your capabilities!
>
> **Jack Ma[1]**

Decisions are the essence of strategic leadership. No matter how good you are at creating a great climate, communicating with clarity or supporting your team, if you make bad strategic decisions then all that work is for nought. As the old adage goes: you can't polish a turd.[2] This is why it is so perplexing that the act of decision making is rarely discussed. Perhaps people think that they are naturally good decision makers. Possibly we are worried about seeming patronising if we talk about decision making with leaders, who, after all, are expected to make a multitude of important decisions daily. Most leadership training on decision making is focused solely on time management. There are some great tools to help you manage your time – for example, the Eisenhower matrix, which is discussed in detail in James Clear's blog.[3] The Eisenhower matrix is broken into quarters based on urgency and importance. Things that are both urgent and important need doing first. Things that are urgent but not important should be considered for delegation. Things that are not urgent but are important need to be scheduled so time is found to complete them. And the final box is non-urgent and unimportant. These should be ignored.

However, I've decided that we will not focus on this aspect. Although time management will crop up in the course of our discussion, as it is vital, I don't think I can add much to what is already available. What I would like to focus on is twofold:

1   The biases that affect the decisions we make.

2   The amount of time we put into each strategy compared to the value it adds to our strategic outcomes.

---

1   Quoted in K. Tan, Billionaire Jack Ma Teaches You How to Be Successful in Life and Business, *LinkedIn* (8 February 2016). Available at: https://www.linkedin.com/pulse/billionaire-jack-ma-teaches-you-how-successful-life-business-tan.
2   For international readers: a turd is poo or faeces.
3   J. Clear, How to Be More Productive and Eliminate Time Wasting Activities by Using the 'Eisenhower Box', *JamesClear.com* [blog] (n.d.). Available at: https://jamesclear.com/eisenhower-box.

Biases we all suffer from

We all suffer from biases. We can't help it. Cognitive biases are the result of faulty thinking. This doesn't mean that you are stupid. By faulty thinking, I mean that in order to cope with the large amount of information our brain has to process, we have naturally developed some shortcuts. These shortcuts lead to certain heuristics or ingrained assumptions that aren't always helpful.

Cognitive biases fall into two categories:

1   **Memory related:** You recall the past incorrectly and use it as the basis for future decisions.

2   **Attention related:** Your attention is a highly sought-after thing, and we are very selective about what we attend to.

Even after reading this you will still suffer from biases and fallacies that will make you lean towards certain pieces of information more than others. Hopefully by being more aware of this you can notice biases in yourself and others and learn to acknowledge and counteract their influence when needed. There are hundreds of notable and named cognitive biases. We are going to focus on a small sample which are most relevant to making decisions under pressure. For each bias I will give an example and afterwards we will discuss ways of avoiding them.

Egocentric bias: 'The older I get, the better I was.'

This one is significant for middle leaders in schools. Egocentric bias occurs because we have too high an opinion of ourselves and our perspective. Essentially, this offers us a slightly rose-tinted view of our own history, implying that we were not quite as good as we think we were. This creeps into leaders' decisions all the time. As they become further removed from the classroom, they find it harder to recall the truth about being a full-time teacher and remember it as being easier than it was. This can lead to overestimating a full-time teacher's capacity to perform the tasks asked of them within a working week.

Example: A senior leader argues in favour of teachers issuing a complex slip for lateness, claiming, 'I would have been able to do it while taking the register and while the students were doing the starter.'

Confirmation bias: 'I knew I was right all along.'

Possibly the most well-known cognitive bias, confirmation bias is the process by which we subconsciously look for evidence that supports our opinion or position. This manifests in us providing ourselves with selective information which supports our initial idea. This can seriously impact subjective judgements – for example, regarding the quality of teaching.

Example: Scanning a spreadsheet of data and only noticing the poor metrics for a teacher who you are convinced is performing poorly based on a snapshot of a lesson you saw.

Anchoring: 'They are about as good as I expected.'

Anchoring is the process by which an initial piece of data influences how all other information is evaluated. Once the anchor is set, decisions are made from that high or low starting point, making it harder to get to the truth. This explains the effect of prior ability data on a teacher's expectations. Even if you think that you treat all students the same, you will subconsciously lower your expectations if the data says a class is low ability.

Example: A student gets a high grade 5 in a mock, but you enter them for foundation tier because their target is a 3.

Authority bias: 'They are the boss so they must know what they are talking about.'

We all have a built-in understanding of hierarchy. Authority bias means you value the thoughts of an authority figure above those of a subordinate. Authority bias from you combined with egocentric bias from your line manager can lead to very bad decision making.

Example: Agreeing to adopt the marking policy your line manager used in their previous school, even though a team member has said that it will not be as effective as the existing policy.

Action bias: 'At least I am doing something about it!'

Action bias is the urge to do something – anything – when a problem is identified. It results in people favouring any action – good or bad – over continuing along the same path. 'If you do what you always do, you get what you always got', is often said as a rebuttal to this, but the key issue here is that some unhelpful actions will be prioritised. This happens in teaching a lot. We always seek to reform and adapt, often missing an important part of the change cycle: embedding a strategy.

Example: Students did not answer essay questions as well as you would have liked, so you replace all the essay-writing lessons in your new scheme of work.

Feature positive effect: 'You don't know what you don't know.'

Due to limited cognitive resources, we prioritise our focus on things that are present rather than considering what is absent. This can lead to ignoring possible negative aspects of the choice because we can't currently see them. This happens all the time when school systems are built. Discussions focus on what features are present in a system, without critiquing things that might be absent, and this leads to short-sighted policies that fail once enacted.

Example: When discussing the new behaviour policy, you spend hours debating the language around uniform infractions without recognising that it is not explicitly clear what happens if an unknown student refuses to give a staff member their name.

Sunk-cost fallacy: 'Throwing good money after bad.'

We demonstrate a greater tendency to stick at things we have invested time, money or effort into. Ideas change in teaching all the time. If you have devoted lots of time and energy to a strategy that is not working, you might be convinced that the best thing to do is invest more time and energy to make it work. This might not be the best decision (as we saw with the idea of opportunity cost).

Example: Last year you invested in a technology platform to assess students' understanding during the lesson using quizzes. After a while you realise mini whiteboards are easier but continue to use the technology as it was very expensive.

How can we overcome our biases?

These are only a sample of the many biases that we suffer from, but fear not, we can overcome. There are several ways to avoid these problems, including using different coloured hats to represent thinking styles. No offence to Mr de Bono, but I am going to recommend two much less flamboyant techniques. The first is simple: try to be aware that you are not perfect and have biases. It sounds obvious, and I'm sure you will want to consider yourself humble and rational, but remember that you are not. The second is to use emissaries. Well, not actual emissaries – there is no need to grant diplomatic immunity or anything. By emissaries I mean representatives from different interested parties. At a department level this could be discussing the idea in principle with a classroom teacher, a fellow leader and your line manager. You could also discuss it with leaders from other departments and support staff – for example, a pastoral leader or a teaching assistant.

Crucially, some of these people must not be closely aligned to you and your principles. You are looking for a mix of dissenting and supportive voices to provide balance to your own thinking. Running an idea past a range of people and really listening to their thoughts is a good way of checking your own thinking. If more than one person keeps bringing up the same issue, don't dismiss it. There is a high chance that they can see something that you cannot right now. The hardest part of this is taking the feedback. It is often very hard to hear critiques of your ideas, especially if they are coming from someone with whom you have historically not seen eye to eye. Work hard to listen and to separate the idea from any value judgements on your character. We will discuss feedback and triggers further in Chapter 8.

When it comes to operational decision making, one of the most powerful tools is John Rawls' veil of ignorance.[4] In this simple thought experiment, which was designed to explore moral decisions, you – the decision maker – are to assume that there is a veil between you and the real world. Behind this veil you know nothing of your standing and context. By doing this you are forced to consider the consequences of your actions on everybody. Behind the veil you could be an NQT, a senior leader or even a student. Doing this helps us to short-circuit our self-serving biases.

As leaders we often fall foul of knowing that the consequences won't affect us as much as others, because we have power to protect ourselves with subsequent decisions. Setting by ability is a simple example. The setting of students has ramifications for all students and staff. When sorting the sets, you have some control over what classes you give yourself. Using the veil of ignorance forces you to make the decision without knowing whether you are teaching the top or bottom set. This obliges you to consider the benefits and drawbacks of different models and come to the best solution for the situation, not for you. Nassim Nicholas Taleb takes this concept further with his idea of skin in the game.[5] The idea is that the more the decision maker is connected to the risks of the decision, the more likely they are to make a good decision. With this terminology, we could argue that the best decision will be made if, instead of not knowing which set we will teach (the veil of ignorance), we assume that we will be teaching the bottom set from the start. That way, we are fully impacted by any negative outcome: truly skin in the game.

---

4   From J. Rawls, *A Theory of Justice* (Cambridge, MA: The Belknap Press, 1971).
5   N. N. Taleb, What Do I Mean by Skin in the Game? My Own Version, *Medium* [blog] (5 March 2018). Available at: https://medium.com/incerto/what-do-i-mean-by-skin-in-the-game-my-own-version-cc858dc73260.

Opportunity cost to impact ratio

How well does something have to be done to achieve a benefit? Consider brushing your teeth. How well do you have to brush your teeth to gain a benefit from it? Does brushing your teeth for two minutes make your teeth twice as clean as brushing for one minute? In middle leadership, time is often the most precious resource. Opportunity cost has been mentioned many times in this book so far, and by now you should have a strong appreciation of its role in everything we do. When you decide on a course of action, do you also agree to what level this needs to be achieved to be effective? Consider the graph in Figure 12, outlining the relationship between the amount of time invested in enacting a strategy and the impact it has.

Figure 12: Time vs impact

This graph is purely theoretical: it has no scale, as different strategies will have varying timescales and potential impact. Essentially, when we enact a strategy, it takes a certain amount of time to get it started. We see this at the beginning of the curve, where the impact lags behind the time axis with a low gradient. The more time we invest, the better the strategy is implemented and the more impact it begins to have, until you get near to optimal implementation. At this point the amount of time needed to increase the impact is much greater as you are essentially trying to get to perfect implementation from the whole team. Figure 13 illustrates this by splitting the time axis into three equal tranches: T1, T2 and T3.

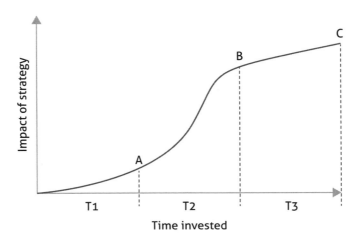

Figure 13: Tranched time vs impact

In the example above, we can see that doubling the time investment from A to B gains us a huge improvement, but the final third has significantly less impact. Sometimes strategies are only effective if they are completed to nearly 100% of their potential. I think that behaviour management policies fall into this category: they need time and energy to get everyone on exactly the same page as consistency is key. If cracks appear then they will drastically reduce the effectiveness. So, for a school's behaviour policy, our line will look as it does in Figure 14: you have to go all in to get the maximum benefit.

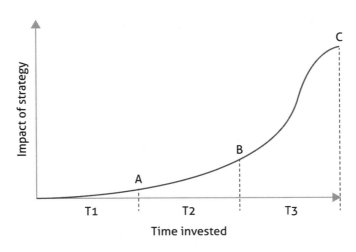

Figure 14: Time invested in behaviour management strategies vs impact

This is not the case for all decisions, however. Often as leaders we want to see our ideas come to fruition completely, to see our magnum opus realised. Unfortunately, we often don't have the time to achieve the perfect version of each strategy. Consider something like retrieval practice. There are many resources available, either for free or at a relatively small cost, that are decent. The training requirement is also low, so our line might look more like it does in Figure 15, and getting to point A in the first year might be going far enough.

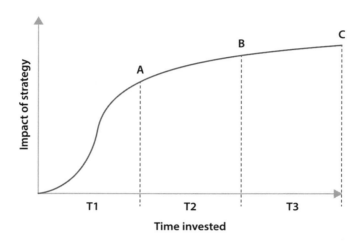

Figure 15: Time invested in retrieval practice vs impact

How well would you have to embed retrieval practice in your team to get most of the benefit? Would you get a similar benefit from using a simple bank of questions as you would from planning each question set into your scheme of work? The second option allows you to ensure that prior knowledge is perfectly interwoven, but the first version is probably good enough and is much quicker from a planning perspective. The time saved can be used to do something else which adds more value than the small increase in retrieval practice would offer. In the case of retrieval practice, it is more important to go from 0% to 60% than from 60% to 90%. The time savings can be spent on something else – for example, getting students to complete their homework or improving the subject knowledge of your team.

Delegation

All leaders need people they can rely on to help them achieve their aims. Often leaders who constantly try to do everything themselves sooner or later burn out. More than that, just like a parent who smothers their children and does everything for them, a leader who is the be all, end all within their team creates a team that lacks initiative and is frustrated by the lack of opportunity to expand their skills and play a valued role. Delegation is often thought of as a leader dumping work onto their underlings but, done well, this could not be further from the truth. By trusting staff and giving them opportunities to take ownership, you are showing how much faith you have in their skills and allowing them to gain valuable experience for self-development.

A good leader is like the rising tide; they should aim to lift all boats. Having said that, again the real world encroaches on our ideals and we must accept the fact that our team members will possess a variety of skills and competencies. Some will be highly suited to doing some tasks with complete autonomy. They will hit a deadline and produce the work to the desired standard with very little oversight. Others will find it hard to organise their time and fail to hit deadlines if left to their own devices. So, we need to vary our degree of delegation. The autonomous team members can be given a very loose form; they just need clear instructions and a deadline and then they can get on with it. They will work on the task and produce the finished article on time and fulfilling the brief. It is worth noting, however, that you need to be prepared for this finished article to not exactly match the image you saw in your mind. Loose delegation affords staff the ability to interpret the task in their own way and this will cause the project to change. This can have benefits, as they might be able to find creative solutions that you haven't seen. It also provides them with a greater sense of ownership and can provide further opportunities for them to expand their leadership experience. Unfortunately, sometimes this can lead to people taking a project in the wrong direction. This risk can be reduced by holding a couple of informal discussions about progress at key times to check that they have understood the brief.

At the other end of the spectrum is the tightest of delegation. In this case, you take ownership of the team members' delivery of the project and the schedule. You will find it best to break down the task into many smaller chunks, each with its own deadline – much like we might approach a task with our students. You will need to devote time to discuss the project at regular intervals and check that it is progressing. One of the advantages of this is that you have a much higher degree of control over the final outcome as you can give regular feedback and direction. The main disadvantage for you is the extra time involved.

There is a potential disadvantage for the team members as well. From the outside you could think this approach would be bad for staff morale as it is potentially quite draconian and stifles the team members' autonomy. However, this is not inherently a function of tight delegation, but of the way in which the work is delegated. If the work is delegated in a very coercive way, with the implication that it is happening because the team member is not good enough to complete the task independently, then it is going to have a negative effect on their morale. But that is due to the way in which you handled it. Tight delegation can be delivered in a way that is warm and supportive. 'I have a really important project that I want to work with you on. It's quite large so I've broken it down into smaller tasks so we can keep track of it. What do you think of these potential deadlines? Shall we meet to review it in a few weeks?' Often when working with people it is not what you do, but the way that you do it.

I felt this distinction first-hand early on in my career. Our head of department had been advised to create a spreadsheet outlining all the time we had gained once Year 11 were on study leave (ah the good old days!). On the surface this makes sense; you want to try to balance the work that needs doing between teachers with extra capacity in a fair way. Back then accountability was all the rage in leadership, and the spreadsheet became a micromanagement to-do list. Soon every hour of gained time was allocated to a specific number of tasks and weekly checks were in place for all staff.

This backfired in a major way. The staff who were quite capable of producing the work and meeting their deadlines felt patronised and mistrusted. Those who did need short deadlines and tight delegation felt panicked and pressured. The leader was spending all their time checking whether other people were meeting their deadlines instead of actually contributing to the department workload. In the end, the work that did get completed was shoddy and morale was low.

In reality, your team will sit somewhere on the delegation continuum shown in Figure 16.

Loose   Tight

✓ Less
   time-consuming
✓ Builds trust

✓ Greater quality
   control
✓ Supports those
   who find it hard to
   manage time

✗ More variation in
   product

✗ Time-consuming
✗ Can erode morale
   if performed the
   wrong way

Figure 16: The delegation continuum

For different kinds of tasks you will need to move to different ends of the spectrum based on your team members' skills and natural propensities. This is a classic example of a good leader knowing their team and learning from previous experiences. You will not always make the right decision but, as a general rule, it's easier to start tight and loosen up as a team member demonstrates their ability to be autonomous.

Getting the most out of meetings

I'm sure you have some horror stories about meetings. I think the old adage 'If you are a manager and bored, have a meeting' is probably a truism for most teachers too. When you hear colleagues discussing their stories of bad meetings, they often talk of those which lasted way too long, those which were short but completely unnecessary and, worst of all, those which were too long and completely unnecessary. I find it strange that, considering we all have these stories, when we become leaders we quickly fall into the same trap. I think this happens for a few reasons.

Firstly, I think this is a decent example of a fundamental attribution error. Essentially, when we become leaders, we think that the leaders we had earlier in our careers held long meetings because they wanted the spotlight and were on a vanity quest, whereas we want long meetings because this issue is important and everyone needs to discuss it. Secondly, I think this is because leadership training encourages the idea of building consensus to secure buy-in from a team. While there is some value in this, I'm confident that a meeting is unnecessary if consensus is not required for a particular decision.

> **Fundamental attribution error:** We judge other people's transgressions as character flaws, but when we are in a similar situation, we attribute our poorer decisions to the context in which we find ourselves.

What are meetings for?

Before we look at how to get the most out of meetings we need to consider if the meeting should take place at all. Why do we need to meet? The most important purpose of meeting as a team is to gain input from a range of people and discuss possible plans of action. Meeting together allows for discussion, debate and solutions from a range of perspectives. The second most important purpose is to seek clarity. Clarity is vital for a successful team. Each member needs to know what we are doing, why, and how they fit in. Clarity regarding an agreed standard or process is crucial. However, clarity can be obtained in many other ways.

Time is a person's most precious resource, but often this is forgotten. Before we arrange a meeting, we need to consider whether what we want to talk about is actually worth discussing. We should ask ourselves:

- Can the people in the meeting really change what is going to happen?
- Do you need everyone to discuss the idea or is it only a few whose input you need?
- Is a meeting the only way for this message to be communicated effectively?

Unless the answer to all three questions is a resounding *yes*, don't have a meeting.

It is worth noting that a meeting is not the same thing as a subject-specific CPD session. Just because a meeting is calendared doesn't mean it has to happen. If you need to fulfil various directed time allocations, hold a co-planning session instead. Everyone can tell if you are just filling time and no one will thank you.

If you answer *no* to any of our three questions, there are plenty of other ways in which to communicate the information. Dr Chris Baker has strong feelings about this.[6] Often the default medium is email. Email is great for notices and policy changes – things that are important but don't need back and forth discussion. Email is clunky for discussion; you end up with multiple reply-alls from everyone clogging up your inbox. Chris' suggestion is that a better tool for discussion is some sort of instant messenger app. Instant messaging software – for example, Microsoft Teams, Slack and WhatsApp – is useful to ask if anyone is free to pick up some printing or where everyone wants to go for the staff Christmas dinner. It is also great for urgent messages, providing staff have enabled notifications. Judicious use of email and instant messaging channels allow you a tiered approach, meaning you can allocate different levels of importance and awareness.

My department has a Microsoft Teams channel that is for general queries. It sends notifications but is considered non-urgent. We also have an urgent channel, and I have set up notifications for this one on my phone. This is where we share things that need attention ASAP, which might involve missing supply teachers, behaviour incidents, etc. Finally, we have a department WhatsApp group which is for all the flotsam and jetsam, memes, photos of your kids, social discussions, etc. Nearly everyone in the department is a member but, crucially, it's not run by me and people don't get offended if someone doesn't reply for a while or has it muted. Team members are in control of their level of engagement. Email is kept for the important issues and things that people will need to reread – exam arrangements, news about the science fair, policy changes, etc.

If we need to roll out a policy and ensure clarity from all staff, my preference is to send it via email and welcome any questions via reply. Then I offer a time window in which staff can come to discuss any questions or concerns with me if they choose. After this, I send out a second email which contains a summary of all the useful questions, and the answers, so all are aware and have a copy for reference. A secondary benefit of this is that it allows team members to take their time absorbing the information. We reduce the chance of cognitive overload and staff can ask questions without the perceived risk of sounding foolish.

---

6   C. Baker, We Need to Talk About E-mail and Meetings: Planning Your School's Internal Communication, *Medium* [blog] (14 May 2020). Available at: https://medium.com/@chrisbakerphysics/we-need-to-talk-about-e-mail-and-meetings-planning-your-schools-internal-communication-db1257ce91de.

How to structure a meeting

Now we know we definitely need a meeting, and it is calendared, so we need to plan for it. If you want meaningful discussion, you'll need a pre-release. A pre-release is a proposal or summary of options for discussion. If you don't start with a proposal, then the discussions will veer off track and time will be wasted. If you want to meet to discuss mock exams, send out the proposed structure and marking schedule in advance, along with the agenda for the meeting. The agenda doesn't need to be a lengthy or formal one; it might just be a few bullet points. Crucially it needs to establish three things:

1   The date, time and location of the meeting.

2   The aim of the meeting.

3   Who will minute the meeting.

I prefer to use a rota so everyone takes a turn doing the minutes. On the day of the meeting, print the pre-release. Yes, staff should have read it, but some won't have – and this way everyone can use it to make notes. Be there early. It's a chance for the early birds to have a quick chat with you and bring up any issues. You can often nip items of any-other-business (AOBs) on the head early. Always have biscuits – at least, that's my opinion. Everyone deserves access to a treat after a long day teaching.

Start on time. Some will be late for valid reasons; others will be late because they were chatting while making a cup of tea. If lateness becomes habitual, it's impossible to shift. Signal your expectations by starting on time.[7] When managing the meeting, engage your teaching skills: keep your explanations clear and concise, break into smaller groups for discussion and circulate. I've been in a lot of meetings in which the chair claims to want discussion but does three things that hamper it:

1   They talk a lot at the start, which makes everyone passive.

2   They try to hold a discussion as a whole group, which makes the stakes of the conversation too high, and as a consequence those half-ideas or questions never get aired.

3   They try to answer each discussion point instead of facilitating others to join in.

It is much easier to visit smaller groups and answer questions as you go. Then bring the groups together again to discuss the salient points, allowing each group to discuss their ideas and challenge your position and each other's. (In Chapter 8 we will talk more about

---

7   Obviously, there is the caveat that you need to pick a sensible time to start the meeting, so you don't shoot yourself in the foot.

building candour and how to appreciate the challenges that others provide.) Don't assume that your idea is the best and don't take it personally if others challenge it. At the end of the meeting, summarise the decisions and next steps. Then it's AOB time. Don't be afraid to cut someone off and offer to discuss with them privately if the issue isn't relevant to everyone. There is no point holding everyone up because Bob's interactive whiteboard is not calibrated. Of course, this can be a chance for others to bring up anything that has slipped through the net. I have found that by structuring meetings in this way they are shorter and more effective, and staff are fully engaged in them.

Budgets and bills

School budgets are strange things. At a central level there is a large amount of money that the school receives based on per-pupil funding. Schools have large overheads, so most of that budget is allocated towards staffing costs. A very small amount is given to each department as capitation. This will vary from department to department, depending on the subject. So art might get more money than history due to the need to buy equipment and supplies. Schools also earmark pots of money for certain projects – say, CPD, literacy, sports provisions, etc. As a leader you might be responsible for your department's capitation. If you have a smaller area of responsibility, then you might be able to request a slice of the capitation to fund projects that you wish to pursue.

The two most important things to know about capitation are that it is very hard to know exactly how much money you have left at any given time and that you can't save some from the previous year and carry it over easily.[8] It's best to try to keep track of your expenditure informally and then check that against the finance office's records termly. By far the biggest departmental expenditure is printing and photocopying, and different schools have different strategies.[9] Some give smaller capitation, but copying is free; others give more money to departments but charge for copying. If you are charged for copying it is absolutely vital that you devise a strategy to get on top of these costs. Uncontrolled, this will eat through most of your capitation and leave you with very little for anything else. Again, this comes down to a careful balancing act. The easiest solution is to allocate how much copying can be done by each teacher. You could issue blanket rules like 'no more than three sides of A4 per student per lesson', but this ignores the fact that copying, if done right, can significantly support the students by ensuring that they are well resourced. A blanket rule might not be the most effective strategy. Another way

8   While not impossible to carry over, it requires the school to be in a surplus budget and often this is not the case.
9   For ease from this point on, assume that if I say 'copying', I mean printing and photocopying – anything that uses ink and paper and gets you the worksheets and so on that you need.

would be to get the majority of your copying completed centrally and store it for use through the term. This way the day-to-day costs are low, but flexibility is reduced. I like to provide a certain amount of copying centrally, in the form of booklets, and then keep an eye on individual staff and have conversations with any who appear to be a bit trigger-happy at the copier.

What if you don't have enough cash?

Sometimes you have a really good idea for a strategy that you want to try but you know that the budget will not stretch. In these situations, you need to go cap-in-hand and sell your idea to someone with a larger pot of money. If it is something that could help teaching and learning across the whole school, then you might be able to put a proposal together and ask your SLT to support it. If it involves technology, you could make a case to whoever oversees the ICT budget. Curriculum changes might allow you to petition for resources from a central pot. If all else fails, you can ask your head teacher or principal. They often have discretionary funds for a rainy day, which they might be able to dip into. Due to the nature of budgets it is often better to ask in the summer term for what you'll want next September, as people are more aware of how much money they have left and are more willing to part with it. Whatever your project is, just ensure that you emphasise its long-term gains and potential applications across the school. If the well is dry, sometimes you can find external sources of money. Depending on your intake demographics there are several external funding sources available. These normally have strict criteria about what they are to be spent on, so take care to ensure that you meet the criteria and can evidence impact at the end.

Recap

- Leaders have to make strategic decisions all the time.
- Leaders, like all humans, suffer from biases that make it hard to make decisions objectively.
- We can overcome our biases by increasing our awareness and employing some simple strategies.
- Once we have made a decision, we also need to consider to what level we need it to be implemented.

- All decisions have opportunity costs, so we have to choose the amount of time and resources to invest in each strategy.

- Meetings are a vital way of communicating with your team and gathering their feedback, but they have consequences, including an opportunity cost.

- Technology can sometimes provide ways to communicate which avoid using staff time and actually improve communication.

- Running a budget is a difficult task. It is important that you keep a close eye on your team's finances and ensure that your strategies are cost-effective.

- Some strategies might need external funding and it's important to emphasise the whole-school impact of these if applying to the principal or to external agencies.

Reflect

- Who are my emissaries?

- How can I avoid my own biases?

- How do I react to criticism of my ideas?

- Do I communicate with my team efficiently?

- Are our meetings efficient? How can I make them more efficient?

- What do I currently spend our budget on? Does it support my vision?

- What are the best sources of extra funding for our projects?

Chapter 7
Pastoral issues

Data – feelings aren't positive and negative. They simply exist. It's what we do with those feelings that becomes good or bad.

Counsellor Deanna Troi, USS Enterprise NCC-1701-D[1]

Why is there a chapter on pastoral issues?

Everyone has a pastoral role within a school. You could be a tutor or have a break duty, for example. Many schools give middle leaders positions of pastoral responsibility. As a middle leader you will have to deal with parents and students regularly, and will need to provide pastoral support. The idea that everyone can do this based on experience permeates teacher training, but learning on the job is incredibly challenging in the high-stakes area of pastoral care. This can lead to inconsistency of practice and leaders feeling ill-prepared to deal with incidents as they occur and when emotions run high. This chapter aims to outline both the mundane and exceptional situations in which middle leaders might find themselves.

Dealing with students in corridor situations

Most of the time, the majority of students are using corridors for their intended purpose and trafficking from one location to another. Sometimes, though, students congregate in corridors and decide to have a heated discussion or a bit of play fighting. Sometimes they behave inappropriately or are late to lessons. Different schools have different ways of handling these situations. I think it is important as middle leaders that we establish some approaches which will help you to successfully intervene with these students to stop them misbehaving and get them to lessons on time.

....

1 *Star Trek: The Next Generation*, Season 6, Episode 26, 'Descent' (1993).

Becoming a middle leader also comes with a step up in other expectations. You are often asked to take a more active role in whole-school systems. You might have increased lunch and break duties, or your school might have a rota of on-call staff to support teachers who have issues with students in their classrooms. Whatever the context, there will be an expectation that you will support your colleagues and challenge students who are not complying. The question then becomes how to challenge a student in an effective way. It's incredibly easy to do this badly.

Before we get into the nuts and bolts of it, I do want to acknowledge that this is not for everyone. Some teachers don't care about the outcome. Their attitude is 'well, the student should just do the right thing', and at a superficial level that is completely true. By learning more about how to talk to students in these scenarios, my hope is that we will try to enable interactions in which the rules are enforced but staff and students maintain, or even build, a positive working relationship. We are trying to get them to do the right thing – both now and moving forward. It's my personal belief that during most corridor conversations with students, if we manage them right, we can not only get them to comply but also to thank us afterwards!

What follows are some simple steps for dealing with corridor altercations. You might already know this from experience, but it is worth reviewing:

- Punish in private. Get the student away from their peer group or it's basically pointless trying to engage with them.

- Challenge the behaviour, not the student. You're just doing your job.

- Get three yeses. Ask three semi-rhetorical questions to which they will inevitably say 'yes'. This builds momentum and agreement. Some classics are 'Do you know the school rule around X?' 'Do you know the sanction for X?' 'I've listened to your side of the story, haven't I?' etc.

- Frame the positive. 'Next time I see you I want to be able to say well done for getting it right.' Or, if they are normally doing the right thing, 'Come on. We both know you are better than this.'

Now I want to delve a bit deeper into the way in which we talk to students, the way in which they respond to us and what we can do to enhance these conversations.

Transactional analysis: why we should talk to students like adults

Transactional analysis is a psychoanalytic technique invented by Eric Berne in the 1950s.[2] We will not be looking at it in great detail, but it has value in helping us to understand how the way in which we talk to people might affect how they respond to us. At a basic level, transactional analysis states that all people, regardless of their age, have three ego states: parent, adult and child.

1 **Parent.** This state comes in two forms. The critical parent is authoritarian and judgemental, while the nurturing parent is reassuring, supporting and understanding. Berne believed that this state was defined by your relationship with your own parents (well, it is psychoanalysis after all!).

2 **Adult.** This state is calm and rational. It is focused on the here and now, confident and non-judgemental.

3 **Child.** There are three categories in this state. The free child that can bring energy, joy and wonder – think of a 6-year-old on Christmas morning. The rebellious child is defiant and complaining – think stroppy toddler or teenager, willing to salt the earth and damn the consequences. Then, finally, there is the adapted child, who is passive and compliant.

Ego state: A consistent pattern of emotion and experience related to a pattern of behaviour.

---

2 E. Berne, *Transactional Analysis in Psychotherapy* (New York: Grove Press, 1961).

Figure 17 outlines various ego states and uses an example of a child with dirty hands to illustrate what each one looks like in a simple transaction.

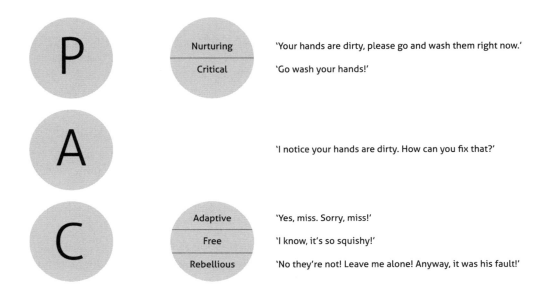

Figure 17: Ego states according to transactional analysis

The utility of transactional analysis is not in these ego states. For me, the power is in how different people communicate in these states and how we respond to them. In an ideal world, we would be communicating via complementary transactions. We would respond in the appropriate ego state to match the one communicated to us. In Figure 18 (see page 127) we have a complementary transaction between two adult states.

Complementary interactions can also occur between parent and child states – for example, 'You've got pen on your hand, go and wash it off, please.' 'Yes, miss.' This also works the other way around, although I don't think that would be common in the school environment.

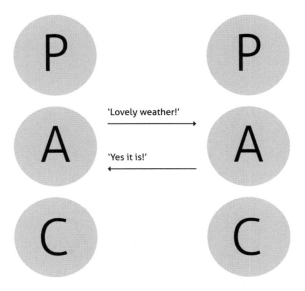

Figure 18: A complementary adult transaction

The problem with parent–child complementary transactions

In a school you have a wide variety of children. These children have wide-ranging relationships with their parents. Often when teachers use a parent ego state, they will receive
a child ego state that corresponds to that child's relationship with their parent or carer. In
early years settings this is less of a problem, but as students get older it can cause issues.
Teachers can elicit the surprising reaction of a rebellious or free child state from an
apparently innocuous sentence. So teachers should aim to assume the adult ego state as
much as possible.

Cross transactions

Cross transactions occur when a person tries to invite a certain ego state and the receiver
refuses to comply. These are more disruptive when between parent and child states.
When a teacher reprimands a student in a scornful tone, they are adopting a critical parent state, usually with the aim of the student adopting an adaptive child state and
accepting that they are wrong. Often, especially in the secondary context, the student will
refuse to adopt that submissive state and instead match the critical parent state. Figure
19 (see page 128) shows a classic example of this phenomenon.

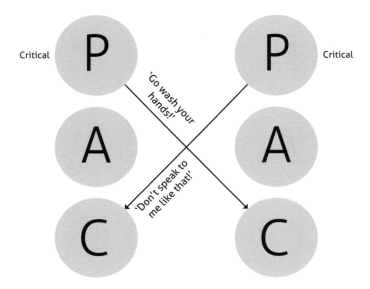

Figure 19: A cross transaction

This often manifests in the students splitting hairs or trying to take some form of offence. They do this to take the initiative and avoid having to address the initial problem or accept responsibility. The best way of avoiding cross transactions is to use the adult ego state as often as possible. Sometimes this requires you to master your own emotions and keep an objective and depersonalised approach. I know, it is easier said than done!

Ulterior transactions

Ulterior transactions appear to come from one state but what is said is actually communicated in a different state. We know that students can tell the difference between what we appear to say and what we mean. A classic example is sarcasm. When we fall into sarcasm, we might believe that we are using the adult state, but really we are using the child state. It is no surprise then that when we are sarcastic to students we can often be met with an escalation of aggression (critical parent) or increased disruption (rebellious child). It's well known that sarcasm is not helpful, and with a basic understanding of transactional analysis we can understand why.

How to get a cross transaction back to an adult–adult transaction

The most important features of the adult state are its focus on the present and its ability to be rational. If we are in a conversation with a student and they are attempting to create a cross transaction, we need to use these two properties to try to bring them in line with our adult state. We can do this by:

- Focusing on the issue at hand, not the future or the past. Every time they start talking about past issues or future consequences, calmly bring them back to the issue.

- Depersonalise the situation. Let them know that you are acting in this way because it is part of your job and that you want them to be the best version of themselves. People make mistakes but they should always have opportunities to put things right. A good tip here is to move from statements of blame – 'You threw that rubber' – to statements of fact – 'I noticed you throw that rubber'. This prevents the 'Why didn't you tell X off? They did it first!' defence and avoids the accusation of you picking on them or not liking them – a classic line that students sometimes use to avoid responsibility.

Putting this all together: what does it mean for us as leaders?

While far from a cast-iron system, transactional analysis provides us with some practical actions we can use when dealing with students:

- We must avoid falling into parent states when talking to students.

- We must avoid sarcasm.

- When faced with a cross transaction, we need to try to move the recipient to an adult–adult transaction.

- We can adopt a nurturing parent state only if the student presents a free or agreeable child state. This might occur more often in primary education. We should be aware of older students using this as a way of avoiding dealing with the consequences of their actions.

The Ben Franklin effect

The Ben Franklin effect is named after the president who wrote in his autobiography of an 'old maxim': 'He that has once done you a kindness will be more ready to do you another, than he whom you yourself have obliged.'[3] This maxim has also been proven by psychologists and demonstrated in experiments.[4] Essentially, the theory goes that if you do someone a favour, you are more likely to do them a second favour. There are different explanations as to why this happens but, really, it's inconsequential for us: we just need to take advantage of it. The best way to get students to do you the first favour is to ask them to move towards you. If you can get them to step towards you, not only are you separating them from their audience, but you are also increasing your chances of getting them to comply with your next request. Sometimes they don't move, sticking instead to their guns. So, walk 90% of the way towards them, while gesturing to the side and calling them over. Then ask their peers to leave. When on their own they will be more likely to take that last 10%.[5]

The familiarity switcheroo

One of the harder aspects of dealing with corridor issues is a lack of familiarity with the students. In a big school it is incredibly hard to know all of the students. If you know the student, you can draw on your pre-existing rapport. You can say things like 'I know you know what the right thing is' or 'This behaviour is very unusual for you. What is going on?' This is not possible if you don't recognise the student. The thing to remember is that this works both ways. Don't pretend that you know them and definitely don't compare them to a sibling who you do know. These are two routes that will often exacerbate the situation. Instead, you can use your ignorance of their reputation as a way of building rapport. 'Look, I don't know you. I can only go on how you are behaving right now. From my perspective, it seems ...' This way, you can use the situation to your advantage. There might be another name for this, but I call it 'the familiarity switcheroo'.

3 B. Franklin, *Autobiography of Benjamin Franklin*, Project Gutenberg ebook edn (New York: Henry Holt and Company, 1916). Available at: https://www.gutenberg.org/files/20203/20203-h/20203-h.htm.
4 J. Jecker and D. Landy, Liking a Person As a Function of Doing Him a Favour, *Human Relations*, 22(4) (1969): 371–378.
5 Obviously this is not 100% guaranteed, but it is the best bet.

Dealing with parents and guardians

Sometimes in leadership you have to deal with parents. You will encounter as broad a range of parental attitudes as you do students. The angry ones will have two main methods of communication: phone and email. There is a third method, which is public shaming of the school via social media, but this is a high-profile incident and should be passed up to the SLT. Often, parents will be angrier via email than by phone. I've always preferred to try to arrange a face-to-face meeting, but for that to happen you have to make contact via email or phone. Sometimes you can't do this right away, either because you do not have the capacity or because you are also angry at the situation. You don't want to deal with the situation when you are angry, but you should always respond and say that you will contact them tomorrow. A simple message, along the lines of 'Thank you for your concerns. I will need some time to investigate this matter. I will contact you within the next 48 hours. Kind regards …' normally does the trick. Finding the best way to deal with these scenarios is not easy. It is perhaps more helpful, in this case, to look beyond the school setting and find an industry that has more frequent dealings with angry or emotive calls.

The best advice for dealing with angry parents – perhaps unsurprisingly – comes from call centres. Below are some guidelines for how best to defuse these situations and start a constructive conversation. I have gleaned these insights from a colleague, Amelia Hitchmen, who spent the first five years of her career working in customer service for a travel insurance company:

- Stay calm. They are angry and probably wrong. Don't take it personally. Remain calm and even-toned in your responses.

- Actively listen. Beneath the anger is a real issue that has made them feel this way. It could be that they have their facts wrong or have been misled by their child.

- Be empathetic. Make it clear that you understand why they are upset. This is not the same as saying that they are right to be upset. However, it may be pertinent to issue an apology if there appears to be fault on the side of the school.

- Get the facts. Ask questions to clarify who said what, where, when, etc.

- Summarise and clarify. Every so often, summarise what you have heard. This gets them to reflect on the facts. When people are angry, they often display the affect heuristic, meaning their thinking processes are ruled by their emotional state rather than their rational thoughts.[6]

6   K. Cherry, The Affect Heuristic and Decision Making, *Verywell Mind* [blog] (7 May 2020). Available at: https://www.verywellmind.com/what-is-the-affect-heuristic-2795028.

- Thank them. Make sure that you thank them for bringing the matter to your attention. While they might not have delivered it in the best way, their feedback will give you information that might help you improve your team.

- Explain the steps you will take and the timescale involved. You might need to arrange a meeting or talk to students. Give the reasons for your decisions. The 'because justification', as it is known, has shown that providing a reason makes a statement more agreeable.[7] Whatever you agree, you must stick to. Trust is a fragile thing.

- Allocate time for follow-up. You need to create time to follow up and check on any agreed actions. There is nothing worse than a parent escalating an issue and your manager discovering that you didn't follow it up.

When it comes to getting a positive result from a parent, I always think that having the student there to explain their perspective really helps – that way you can all reach an agreement and nothing is lost in translation. As a rule, I try to ensure that for every concession I have to make, the student has to make one too. That way you prevent the precedent that if you complain, you get what you want. You don't want word getting round the student body that you are a pushover, resulting in you being inundated with complaints about the smallest of things.

Dealing with a student in crisis

I'm sure we've all been there. The classroom door creaks open with a gentle knock while you are prepping for the next lesson. 'Sorry, sir. Can I speak to you for a moment?' Your heart sinks, you take a deep breath. *Remember your safeguarding training!* Your brain reminds you as you reply, 'Sure, come on in.' Over the last 17 years of being a tutor and a leader I have had my fair share of those moments. In my NQT year a student told me that she was planning on running off to join the circus. This was not actually as weird as it might seem because, as I later found out, her father was a circus performer. These conversations can vary greatly, from mundanely unpleasant things – like relationship break-ups – to the more substantial – like gender transitioning, suicide and substance abuse. Some of the most meaningful work I have ever done has been during these conversations. In Chapter 9 I discuss how to support a staff member in crisis, so if you find a student in tears and unable to continue to work that day, you'll be able to apply that sort of support. For now, let's focus on what happens after the revelatory moment. You have

---

7   E. J. Langer, A. Blank and B. Chanowitz, The Mindlessness of Ostensibly Thoughtful Action: The Role of 'Placebic' Information in Interpersonal Interaction, *Journal of Personality and Social Psychology*, 36(6) (1978): 635–642.

found the issue, and any safeguarding concerns have been logged and actioned. Now you have a student in perpetual crisis or low-level but persistent distress. They must continue to function and will be coming to you for support on a semi-regular basis. I want to start with some dos and don'ts for these situations.

Table 6: Some dos and don'ts for helping students in crisis

Do	Don't
Do care about them. Show empathy and an appreciation of their situation.	Don't overreach your boundaries. It is vital that you maintain distance from the situation. You can be emotionally available to them, but you must maintain some separation, or your decision making will suffer. You are not there to save them; you are there to support them, along with any external agencies.
Do work to help them feel better. Acceptance is key here. Make sure that they know that you know that they are not a bad person.	Don't solve their problems. This will lead to co-dependency and white knight syndrome, whereby they see you as the solution to all their problems and you relish being the saviour. It's a very slippery slope and helps no one.
Do confide in others. While the nature of the issue might be confidential, keep in regular contact with another member of staff who can act as a sounding board and provide a level of support to you if needed.	Don't be passive. Be assertive if needed. Don't be afraid to draw attention to any faults in their thinking or conflicting statements. There is no time to passively wait for them to come to an epiphany.

With some students your job will simply be to listen and provide a place for them to vent. Therapeutic work will be done by professionals if it is accessible. When listening to these students, you might want to follow the guidance in Chapter 9. For other issues that are not serious enough to trigger external agencies, or if those agencies prove ineffective or slow to access, we need a strategy to support the student. My aim here is to give you a broad overview of some aspects of CBT – the idea being that you might be able to use some of these techniques to help the student to move through their crisis.[8]

CBT, at a surface level, is incredibly accessible and adaptable. Its focus on goals and the present situation make it perfectly suited to supporting students, and its structured approach means that it offers you a framework to put in place. According to CBT, most issues can be helped by adjusting thought patterns. The father of CBT, Aaron Beck, came up with the idea that thoughts spiralled in on themselves, thereby affecting the way we perceive our reality. Figure 20 outlines his negative triad.

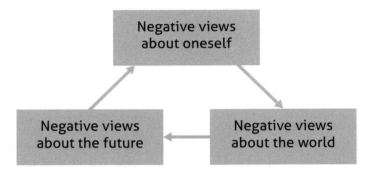

Figure 20: Beck's negative triad

Beck recognised that most negative thoughts come from faulty assumptions: things the person believes to be true but are not – for example, 'no one will ever love me'. Often people are able to keep these negative thoughts in perspective, but incidents can trigger a thought spiral. Thoughts change the person's view of the world, which in turn affects their view of the future. These combine to change the person's behaviour, which often helps to perpetuate the cycle. The aim of CBT is to break this cycle by creating alternative thought processes.

Aspects of CBT can be helpful in supporting our conversations with students. To become an expert in CBT requires training and considerable practice, but here are some of the things we can easily build into our conversations with students:

● **Structure:** Keep a level of formality to the discussion. Agree the duration (45 minutes works well) and frequency of these talks.

---

8   Adapted from United Nations Office on Drugs and Crime, *Leader's Guide: Cognitive Behavioural and Relapse Prevention Strategies*, Treatnet Training Volume B, Module 3 (2007). Available at: https://www.unodc.org/ddt-training/treatment/VOLUME%20B/Volume%20B%20-%20Module%203/1.Leaders%20Guide/Presentation%20-%20VolB_M3.pdf.

- **Problem and goals:** Have the student clearly verbalise the problem and ask them what their goal is in speaking to you (this could just be 'to feel better').
- **Discussion:** Then discuss the problem in relation to situations that arise, the thoughts they have, how these affect their emotions, any physical responses (e.g. raised heart rate) and also how they react. The aim is to begin to make a cause-and-effect link between situations, thoughts and effects.

This process is called functional analysis. Table 7 is an example template for a simple functional analysis that could be carried out together or set as homework.

Table 7: A functional analysis template

Antecedent situation	Thoughts	Feelings and sensations	Behaviour	Consequences
Where was I? Who was with me? What was happening?	What was I thinking?	How was I feeling? What signals did I get from my body?	What did I do? What did other people around me do at the time?	What happened afterwards? How did I feel right after? How did people react to my behaviour? Were there any other consequences?

The template ensures that the conversation covers:

- **Situations that lead to issues:** Can they be avoided? Avoidance is most likely what the student will already be doing. Can that go on forever? Is it a healthy coping strategy? We need them to accept that this situation will occur again.
- **Thoughts:** This is the hard part. Can we get them to vocalise what they think in that situation? Often students just clam up with 'I dunno', so you might need to lead them a bit.
- **Feelings:** Can they recognise the feelings and their physical manifestations? If they begin to feel anxious, can they become aware of the early signs – shallower breathing, heart rate rising, etc. – and acknowledge the feeling?

- **Actions and consequences:** How do they respond to these feelings and thoughts? What are the consequences of their actions? Is this working for them? For example, when some people get angry, they go for a run. This is not really a strategy that needs to change as it does no harm. However, if their response is to pick a fight, then they need to see how this is not productive.

Once you and the student have a more detailed awareness of the problem, now you can inform them of the central edict of CBT: we all have negative automatic thoughts in some situations, but some of us are better at regulating them due to our life experiences. It is really important that the student knows that they are not alone and not to blame. As issues are unpicked and discussed, any strategies should be role played. This can seem forced but it's vital that the new behaviour is seen enacted by a third party and copied so that it can be learnt. Along the way there will be setbacks. It's vital that these are framed as learning experiences. They might suffer from abstinence violation effects, wherein they make one mistake and then assume that they are destined to fail, and so they then quit trying. Lapses are somewhat inevitable, but we must fight to avoid ending back at square one.

Abstinence violation effects: The process by which a person abstaining from a particular substance or behaviour has a relapse. The associated shame is attributed to a personal flaw and used as an example of their inevitable failure. This results in them relapsing back into their old ways.

The final step is to set homework. The student needs to practise a specific strategy to disrupt the triad. This could be situational – for example, if the student struggles with a drug issue, the first step would be to avoid the situations and people normally associated with their drug use. While not a long-term fix, this is a first step.

Other homework could involve them listening for those negative automatic thoughts and correcting them or recognising their anger trying to manage it. Whatever the homework, make sure you give a clear rationale for why it needs to be carried out and how it fits into solving their problem. Stress that it will take lots of practice to make it stick. Often students will come back the following week having not completed their homework (surprise!). Generally, the reasons fall into two categories:

1   'I just didn't do it!' If this is the case, we need to use praise approximations: find the one positive step they did take and emphasise that. A simple one is 'Maybe so, but you turned up today so I'm proud you made that right choice.'

2   'I didn't have time.' If this is the case, we need to overcome the obstacles by changing the homework. 'How can we make the homework easier to do tomorrow?'

Each session will involve reviewing the homework, discussing the difficulties, and deciding what the next steps will be.

Pastoral issues are often ignored in leadership training. However, there are models out there that we can use to try to enhance our conversations with students in a variety of situations. This is by no means a foolproof system and there will be times when things will go wrong no matter how well you follow this advice. I hope that some of these ideas are helpful whatever your role within the school is, because we all have a pastoral responsibility.

Recap

- All teachers have a vital pastoral care role, but leaders have an expanded role and should be aware of how to effectively interact with students in a range of situations.

- Challenging students can be difficult but there are a range of simple techniques we can use to increase the probability of a successful conversation.

- Transactional analysis helps us to understand the ways in which people interact with each other so we can adapt our behaviours to create win-win situations.

- When supporting students who are in crisis there are simple things we can do to help and, if necessary, CBT techniques can provide much-needed support.

Reflect

- How do I challenge students in corridor situations?

- What ego state do I fall into when I am frustrated?

- How comfortable would I be supporting a student in need?

- What other resources are there in my school to help me to support students?

Chapter 8

Leading others

What you permit you promote, what you allow you encourage and what you condone you own.

Anonymous

I have no idea who initially came up with this quote but, whoever they are, I have to be honest and say that I hate them. I hate them so much. I hate them because once you realise the truth of this statement, you can't go back. You can't turn a blind eye so you can nip to the toilet before your lunch duty starts. You can't let that student with black trainers walk past you and you can't ignore a minor gap in a teacher's subject knowledge. You must make a stand. The weight of leadership is significant and unrelenting, which is why the focus of Chapter 9 is on your personal wellbeing.

Whatever your role in middle leadership you will have a team. That could be a team of tutors in a pastoral capacity, a key stage or a subject. If you are the leader of a key stage in a subject, then you don't have exclusive leadership of that team, but you still need to be able to lead in your area of responsibility. Often this is overlooked and people think that they are tied to whatever leadership the head of department provides. This is not true; own your area of responsibility and lead it as you see best.

Your team is unique. It is made of unique individuals and so, by definition, it is one of a kind. That being said, to provide practical guidance we need to generalise. This allows us to look for commonalities and patterns, with the aim of creating some sort of optimal process which leads to team unity and productivity. The main tenet of this chapter is know your team. Try to take the most applicable aspects of this advice to your team and adjust for your context. Think of this chapter less as scripture and more as a series of recommendations.

Department dynamics

There are a lot of different ways to assess the dynamics of your team. Famously, there are the Myers-Briggs Type Indicator (MBTI) tests and the Big Five personality traits. These sorts of personality tests have given rise to a cottage industry within leadership training. I am sure that this – as with so many things – began with good intentions. The aim was to support the interpersonal skills of teachers as they became leaders. I suspect that the idea was to somehow unlock your potential as a leader by decoding your instinctive personality profile. With this knowledge of yourself you can then somehow fix your weaknesses to make you a superhero leader. Then everything will be fine! We then think maybe if we can profile our team, we can gain some sort of cheat code which unlocks them? Maybe Janice will be less of a gossip and Dominic will hit his deadlines if I know they are introverts or have high levels of neuroticism?

We don't have time to debunk this strategy here, but there is lots of writing out there about it. Just looking at it objectively it seems pretty obvious that it's hokum. People are complex and variable. We often demonstrate certain trends over time, but these are approximations. On a given day we can be vastly different. We do have habits, though. Dominic has a habit of being late to complete work. Janice has a habit of gossiping and creating disharmony. These are very separate issues that need dealing with in very different ways. Categorising these individuals according to some arbitrary system doesn't really get us anywhere.

The other danger is that by embracing these tests we promote the idea that there is a certain type of person who makes a good leader. This is dangerous as it excludes a raft of potentially very good leaders from applying for leadership roles. It promotes a sort of personality cult of a mythical ideal school leader — someone who was born to lead and gets results due to their natural charisma and communication skills. This archetype embodies all the adjectives you see describing leaders in job advertisements. Tom Rees and Jen Barker of Ambition Institute surveyed a series of SLT job adverts and pulled out the adjectives.[1] The list contained the following:

- Dynamic.
- Innovative.
- Strong.
- Inspirational.
- Motivational.

1   T. Rees and J. Barker, Expert School Leadership: What Is It and How Might We Get More of It? [video], *researchED Home* (16 May 2020). Available at: https://www.youtube.com/watch?v=g5c6a9kw-3E&t=28s.

- Sensitive.

- Enthusiastic.

- Warm.

- Charismatic.

- Visionary.

- Determined.

Let's pause a second to absorb this list. A few things spring to mind: firstly, just how much of an inflated ego would you need to read it and go 'Hmm, yeah I think I am all these things'? Except the people applying for these roles are not egomaniacs; they have realised that these words are relatively meaningless. I once interviewed for a head of sixth form vacancy. I had been given the school's data for the last five years to evaluate. I had gone on learning walks and provided feedback to teachers from a range of subjects. The interview process seemed to be going well. Then I was asked to predict what I expected the value-added outcomes to be within a year of me taking over the role. I gave a prediction of a modest increase and I did not get the job. In my feedback it was pointed out to me that my modest prediction demonstrated a lack of ambition and determination. I can only assume that the other candidates had given much larger predictions.

I thought the question was about the skill of estimating and projecting forward. I now realise that the question was about blind confidence, displaying ambition and false promises. Needless to say, I felt slightly vindicated that the actual results the following year were similar to my prediction. I tell you this not because I want your pity or derision for being so naive, but to illustrate how this language permeates the recruitment process and impacts upon how decisions are made. It was obviously not the only reason why I was not chosen, but it was clearly a significant factor as it was brought up in the feedback. As Rees points out:

> It's hard to think, isn't it, of a human being who could possibly claim to be all of these things. How could you write a letter of application, for example, with a straight face claiming to be all these different things. It kind of leads us towards the hero paradigm of school leadership. We want this kind of visionary, inspiring characters to lead our schools. And it also doesn't seem plausible that these traits and behaviours necessarily stack up as the most important things that we want the people running our schools to be.[2]

2   Rees and Barker, Expert School Leadership, at 8:21 mins.

This observation really stuck with me. Consider your own experience. If you take the time to consider the leaders in your school, you will probably notice that they are incredibly varied. You should also notice that your opinion of their proficiency and of their personality do not correlate: the ones you value as strong leaders will not all lead the same way.

To understand your department dynamics you need to know your team. You need to spend time with them and observe how they interact with each other. If you are new to the team you can quickly understand the relationships by watching the staff interact. Often a true word is said in jest, so look out for the running gags and jokes. As a new leader it is vital that you get to know the factions within your team and are aware of any pre-existing issues. At the same time, playing ignorant to these divisions is a great way to help break them down and create a more unified team.

Superstars vs rockstars

In *Radical Candor* Kim Scott credits an unnamed Apple executive with this way of describing the two types of people on a great team.[3] Superstars are those who are highly competent and ambitious. They are the hot shots who are itching to take on responsibility and progress throughout their careers. They love to go the extra mile and they provide a driving force for change when their energies are harnessed correctly. They need to know there is a path for them to follow and they are not being held back. They may not be around for long, often looking for that next step on the ladder.

Rockstars are on a slower trajectory of growth. However, they are experts in their own roles. In education, these will be those classroom teachers who enjoy staying in the classroom and just being brilliant on a day-to-day basis. They are not looking for extra responsibility and need to be appreciated if they are to perform at a high level day in, day out. Leaders are often drawn to superstars due to their eagerness to move into leadership themselves. However, teams can't create sustained success if they are all superstars; rockstars provide a bedrock of stability to drive success. They are the foundation that endures and allows others to flourish. Trying to force a rockstar into the role of a superstar often backfires. They often become stressed and unhappy. It is important to find ways to allow your superstars to flourish and your rockstars to feel appreciated. It is important to remember that people are not fixed in each role. Someone might begin their career as a superstar, but after a few years their priorities change and they find that they prefer to be a rockstar for a while. Likewise, rockstars might become superstars as their priorities shift and they find themselves eager to pursue a certain role. During your conversations with

---

3   K. Scott, *Radical Candor: How to Get What You Want by Saying What You Mean* (New York: Macmillan, 2017).

your team you should try to gauge how they see themselves and how you see them. These visions might not align, and you might need to approach decisions you make that contradict their self-perception tactfully. After all, that's why they pay you the big bucks!

Managing change

As leaders, one of the most important things we do is introduce change to a system. Chapter 6 discussed the decision-making processes that go on behind the scenes. As humans, one of the things we are often most resistant to is change, so here we will focus on how to implement the change you want. The way in which we introduce change is going to be key. If we introduce it in an ineffective way, it won't matter how good the idea is, you won't be able to bring your team with you.

You as a leader

The first step to managing change is all about you as a leader. If you are not seen as an effective leader, why would anyone follow you? There are huge amounts of research and writing on what an effective leader is, which is quite strange because leadership is hard to define. Leaders look very different in different domains and use varying techniques. I'm not going to spend time in this book going through the minutiae of different leadership theories. I will just share some of my thoughts on the issue. I think it's important to ask yourself some honest questions. This is not about right and wrong answers; it is more of a tool to ensure self-awareness.

Who do you work for?

Honestly, why do you do the job? Some people work for the students. They become leaders because they want the best for every single student. Others become leaders because they passionately want to help their staff. They want to protect them from the potential negative effects of poor decisions and help them grow. Others are more career driven. They work for their senior leaders first and foremost and aspire to be in their position soon. None of these positions are wrong, but you need to be honest with yourself as it will subconsciously impact how you deliver changes.

Do you have skin in the game?

Do you expose yourself to the risks of your own decisions? Will you walk the walk? Team members can quickly figure out if a leader is willing to roll their sleeves up and get stuck in. If you make a rule that all students who don't do their homework get a phone call home, how many calls are you willing to make? If you say no hot drinks in the classroom, are you willing to leave your mug in the office even though you have not had a brew all day? Leaders who have skin in the game are often described as authentic leaders.

Do you stay the course?

Some leaders are very good at sticking to a plan of action. They show patience when strategies do not show results immediately – although this can, of course, lead to rigidity if taken to the extreme. Others lack conviction in their own strategies and see any early setbacks as a signal that it is all going wrong. While these masters of panic might not be desirable, having the courage to recognise a bad strategy and change course is a very useful skill. Where do you feel you fit on the rigidity–panic spectrum?

Try to honestly reflect on these questions. You might not always be consistent in your answers, but it will help you to recognise your predispositions. If you are not happy with some of your answers, well, the good news is that you are a conscious being and can work to change those habits. Yay for the prefrontal cortex! If the truth differs from your ideal self, you can try to work on that yourself, or you can request some coaching or mentoring. Teams will follow leaders who they know they can trust. If they know that you have their interests in mind, that you have skin in the game and that you are willing to change but not easily panicked, then their trust will be high. If you have their trust, then their morale is high and that's useful because morale is the currency of change.

As a leader you can impose change however you want. Your team will change, or at least appear to change. The question is: how much morale will it cost? If you make a decision that they think is poor, and you do a terrible job of selling it, then the cost in morale is high and performance will definitely deteriorate. This will reduce your ability to introduce further change. Retention of team members might also suffer. A good idea poorly delivered will hit morale over the short term. A bad idea well delivered will hit morale over the long term. Our aim is to make a good decision and deliver the change in a way that costs the least in terms of morale.[4] This is why leadership is often discussed in terms of

---

4   It is possible to gain morale, obviously. A popular idea that makes life better is an easy win, but there is no need for a book on that.

relationships: having strong relationships with your team gives you a larger reserve of morale from which to draw.

The next step is about understanding how people behave. Famously, the world's foremost protector against alien invasion, Agent Kay (Tommy Lee Jones, *Men in Black*), said it best. 'A person is smart. People are dumb, panicky, dangerous animals and you know it.'[5] When preparing to deliver change, we need to understand how humans behave and what that tells us about communicating change to them.

The elephant, the rider and the path

Psychologist Jonathan Haidt has the best analogy for explaining human behaviour.[6] He says that humans are essentially moral creatures who have strong instinctive reactions to things. These are formed over many years from the sum of their experiences and the cultural factors that they are steeped in. Think of it like an emotional schema. This is the elephant: strong, instinctive and single-minded. Humans also have a rational mind that creates meaning and plans. This is the rider atop the elephant, holding the reins. Just like the rider, the rational mind sees itself as the master of the instinctive emotional mind. The problem is that this is not true. The elephant will go wherever it pleases and act according to its instincts. The rider can't do much to stop it. Woe betide anyone who drops a bag of peanuts within 10 feet of an elephant is all I'm saying.

The rider wants to feel in control so will try to steer the elephant in the right direction. Sometimes it works, if the elephant is willing. When the elephant isn't, the rider has a choice to make. They can either admit that they have no control as the elephant veers off into the jungle or they can exclaim loudly, 'Oh, yes, the jungle! That's where I wanted to go anyway!' When the rational mind does this it starts to generate reasons to justify our behaviour. This happens after our emotions have prompted us to act. Haidt calls these post hoc rationalisations. Change spooks the elephant. Once spooked, people will talk their rational mind into resisting the change, even if it is objectively a great idea. When introducing change to your team, you need to communicate to the elephant *and* the rider if you want them to take the change on board.

Chip and Dan Heath have also used this analogy in their book *Switch*.[7] They introduce the idea of the path: the route that is easiest for the elephant to follow. As leaders we now

---

5   *Men in Black*, dir. Barry Sonnenfeld (1997).
6   J. Haidt, *The Happiness Hypothesis: Putting Ancient Wisdom to the Test of Modern Science* (London: Arrow, 2007).
7   C. Heath and D. Heath, *Switch: How to Change Things When Change Is Hard* (New York: Random House Business Books, 2011).

have three avenues of communication that we need to open up in order to get our team to buy into the change with the smallest drop in morale:

1 **The rider:** We need to have a logical reason for change. Start by identifying the driver for change: what is the problem? Make sure that they understand the context without providing a bogeyman (you don't have skin in the game if you blame the tough decisions on your head teacher or Ofsted inspectors). Be clear about the reason why the change is coming, what is going to change and why it's worth the effort.

2 **The elephant:** We need to know how the change might feel. Start by painting a picture of the impact. Focus on the common areas of motivation (students, workload, performance of the team, etc.). Get them to imagine the emotions that they will feel when it works. 'Yes, this will be a change in how we work, but just imagine how the students will feel when they turn up and receive their new mastery booklets. Those students whose parents don't buy revision guides will now have something to take with them to revise at the end of the year … Think about all those hours at the photocopier you will have back.' By reducing bigger changes into smaller chunks and building them up slowly, you can avoid spooking the elephant.

3 **The path:** We need to make change easy. Carefully consider the barriers to change: what needs to be in place first? What can you do centrally to make it easier to do the new thing than keep doing the old? This is often called nudge psychology as it is all about making compliance convenient. At a very basic level this involves having worked examples of new systems ready to demonstrate.

The elephant, the rider and the path: it's the secret to communicating change. We now have communicated the change that we want to happen. We just need to rally the herd of elephants and riders so that they all follow the path together.

The power of the first follower

You can be the best leader in the world but without people to lead you will be pretty pointless. Calling yourself a leader is not enough. Author and entrepreneur Derek Sivers has a great example in his Ted Talk.[8] He likens leading to a solitary man dancing at a music festival, and points to a viral video of a crowd gathering around him as an excellent example of group behaviour. When leading, you have to take risks and put yourself in the path

---

8   D. Sivers, First Follower: Leadership Lessons from a Dancing Guy, *Derek Sivers* [blog] (2 November 2010). Available at: https://sivers.org/ff.

of criticism. People will circle and observe you but they won't follow until they know what to do and that it is safe. For this to happen, we need the first follower. The first follower does two things: they give permission for others to follow without criticism and they model what following looks like. With the first follower, the dancing man now has a partner. Within moments the pair will rise to three and, as we all know, that is officially a crowd. Getting the first follower is incredibly important when engaging a team in a change process. Once you get that first follower, the middle-ground majority will quickly follow. Those reluctant to take up the change will follow slowly; the saboteurs will probably take ages and might never fully follow, but that's just the way life goes.

How do we get that first follower? The easiest way is to target some team members early in the process of strategising and bring them into the fold. Run your idea past them and get their feedback. Then, when you are trialling the strategy, you can get them to try it before you talk to the rest of the team. When you meet the team you can introduce the strategy and invite your first followers to describe their thoughts and some of the advantages. This signals to the rest of the group that the change is not threatening, illustrates what following looks like and calms the elephant's initial response of fear.

Managing up

You can't be a middle leader without having a line manager: it's called middle leadership after all! Your line manager can massively impact the work you do with your team. They can be a hugely beneficial source of experience and advice. They can advocate your needs to the wider school and remove barriers that prevent you from implementing your plans. Unfortunately, they also have the potential to be obstructive and controlling. They can be fixated on what worked for them when they were in middle leadership, or not make time to support you as much as you need. On top of this, they often are not specialists in your subject, which can lead to false assumptions and confusion.

You can't control who your line manager is, but you can manage them and account for their strengths and weaknesses. In my many years of middle leadership I have had line managers who were very tight with their delegation and dedicated large amounts of time and energy to creating and delivering strategies to help me. Other times, my line managers have been much looser with their delegation. This gave me more freedom, but less support. At each end of the spectrum there are ways to make it work. It's important to recognise that you are not going to change them. They have their own proclivities and, as a middle leader, you must work with their disposition to get a favourable result. Managing up – the process of ensuring that your line manager is performing in a way that yields positive results – is something that is often overlooked when discussing middle leadership. It is vital that you identify the way in which your line manager behaves and find strategies to get the most out of your relationship. By adjusting your approach you can make your line management meetings efficient, overcome any potential barriers and build a strong foundation for sustained improvement.

How do we manage upwards? Firstly, it's important to stress that it is not about manipulation. It is about taking some time to consider the strengths and weaknesses of your line manager and to consider what is under your control. Let's start by considering some easy quick wins. They are professional essentials, but it is worth explicitly stating them:

- Be on time – simple.

- Be organised: don't be someone they have to chase to meet a deadline.

- Be positive and supportive – of your team and of your line manager.

- Be open to their input. Even if you don't always agree, their perspective will help consolidate your thoughts.

- Be willing to ask questions. Don't go away and suffer in silence when you don't understand; instead, clarify and check.

- Be willing to be the bearer of bad news. Keep an open dialogue with them so there are no surprises. Much better they know from you if something is wrong than find out from someone else or when the problem escalates.

The questions that follow are a little more nuanced and context dependent, but worth considering:

- What are they an expert in? They are your superior, but they are not necessarily an expert in your subject area. They might have expertise which you lack, and here you can rely on their support. For example, I had a line manager who knew nothing of the science curriculum – so when it came to decisions about routes and assessments their advice was often incorrect – but they did have expertise in organisation and were an excellent source of advice on how to structure the systems in the department to make them simple and effective. They were also highly experienced in improvement planning and self-evaluation – areas in which, at the time, I was a complete novice.

- What can they do to get the best out of you? When in discussion with your line manager, make it clear what you need in order to do your best. Do they need to gently guide you, or do you need someone to give you tight delegation in areas where you are struggling? Often, one of my past line managers did not do a great job of helping me because I wasn't clear about what I needed to be successful, mainly because I lacked the necessary self-awareness at the time.

- What motivates them? Why are they in the job? What got them there? Where do they want to go next? If they rose up the ranks fast due to making significant time commitments and their inherent people skills, then that is going to be their approach to all things. If their organisational skills got them where they are, then that will be their approach. 'To the man with a hammer, everything is a nail.' You will need to be mindful of this.

- How do they make decisions? Some like to talk everything out, so expect them to be at your door suggesting extra meetings. Others will be all about emails. Some will be very directive and others much more collaborative. It might be worth asking 'Is this up for discussion or has the time passed?' Too many middle leaders waste time and energy arguing against changes that have already been decided. Best to try to get ahead of the next decision by emphasising your willingness to be part of the process.

- How do they communicate decisions? Be clear about their mode of communication.

I once got this last point massively wrong. One of my line managers was a fan of the corridor conversation and when we bumped into each other they would invariably bring up a task that needed doing. I listened, but didn't really listen, thinking that it would be confirmed in an email or a meeting. In their mind, they had gone above and beyond by taking the time to find me and had displayed the personal touch by discussing it. Needless to say, an important task to do with the prospectus slipped my mind and I forgot to do it. When the deadline passed, I had the shock of finding out that I had messed up. I think I was up late that night completing the work, so the school didn't miss the print deadline! Now I can look back with years of hindsight and say that that's not a great way to lead, but also, I can see that I learnt a lesson. From that point on, whenever we had these conversations, I would confirm the task later in an email and write it on my to-do list. I wasn't going to change the way my line manager worked – at least, not instantly – so I needed to adapt slightly.

By taking time to consider our line managers' various attributes we can negotiate the path of least resistance and ensure a positive and productive working relationship.

Giving and receiving feedback

If there was ever a sentence that best illustrated the difference between the elephant and the rider it is this statement: feedback is a gift. Yes, we all know in our enlightened rational mind that getting feedback is one of the most effective ways to improve. However, the elephant, that emotional mind, really doesn't enjoy most forms of feedback.

In *Thanks for the Feedback* Douglas Stone and Sheila Heen outline several reasons why feedback can be so hard to hear.[9] If there is a difference in the kind of feedback being given and the kind of feedback desired, then the elephant gets spooked and the feedback washes over the person without truly being heard. If I visit a newly qualified teacher's classroom, I need to be clear about my intended purpose when feeding back my thoughts. If I just offer appreciation, but they are keen to receive coaching, then my simple platitudes come off as demonstrating a lack of care in their development. Conversely, if they are at their wits' end, tired and full of their third cold of the term, my detailed explanation of how to improve participation ratio will not be heard. Aligning your feedback can be achieved by discussing it with them formally. 'I saw some really good things that I'd like to discuss first, then there are a few areas that I'd like to talk about where I think I can help you. How does that sound?' Or you can negotiate this on the fly by paying close attention to their responses.

Feedback delivered as a middle leader will mostly be following lesson visits or learning walks. The learning walk cycle is predicated on the importance of feedback. Feedback should be given in a timely fashion, ideally face to face, focusing both on strengths and areas for development. There are various structures that we are told to use: feedback sandwiches, ping pong and bungees are all commonly touted in training as tools to help us frame the feedback effectively. Although, if I'm being honest, that's not entirely true: one of those I just made up to illustrate how leadership training loves a good gimmick.

As the person delivering the feedback there is one irreconcilable problem that you face: you have no control over how your feedback is received. A teacher can do many things to try to get students to pay attention, but they can't physically force a student to think. Similarly, you can set your conversation up as well as is humanly possible, but that doesn't mean that the teacher will hear your feedback.

---

9   D. Stone and S. Heen, *Thanks for the Feedback: The Science and Art of Receiving Feedback Well* (New York: Penguin, 2015).

Consider the following scenario:

Fade to black

The scene opens in a typical classroom on a typical day. It's lesson 3 and the smell of chips cooking in food tech is wafting down the corridor. The classroom door opens and in walks someone on a learning walk. They smile and, with clipboard in hand, sit at the back of the class. After a while they talk to the students, look at some books and then leave. After the final bell they pop back into the room with their clipboard.

Observer: 'Can I give you some feedback?'

Me: 'Sure.'

Observer: 'I really liked the feel of the class. They seem to like you and you have built strong relationships. They work for you.'

Me: 'Thanks.'

Observer: 'I think to improve you should get the students to just indicate with a show of hands which questions they got right so you can use it to inform future teaching.'

Me: 'OK, thanks.'

Observer: 'But, once again, thanks for having me in and well done.'

End scene

Unfortunately for the observer, this is what I heard:

Observer: 'Can I judge you?'

Me: 'Sure.'

Observer: 'Blah blah blah relationships blah blah blah work blah.'

Me: 'Thanks.'

Observer: 'I don't like the fact that you reject self-report because I like proxies that make me feel good.'

Me: 'OK, thanks.'

Observer: 'Once again, token thanks.'

Now, you might be reading this and thinking several things:

- What an honest and brave admission of a problem we all have but never admit to – bravo!

- Wow! What an ungrateful idiot.

- I never do that.

- People listen to my feedback because I care and make sure it's the best it can be.

- What's wrong with self-report?[10]

Whatever your thoughts, one thing should be clear: the observer had no control over how I was going to take their feedback on that day. I don't always take it this badly, but sometimes I do. And so do you.

The word 'feedback' can mean three different things. When someone asks for feedback they could be asking for:

1 **Appreciation:** some words of encouragement.

2 **Evaluation:** an indication of how they are performing.

3 **Coaching:** advice about how to improve.

There is a caveat here: coaching has an element of evaluation built into it. You can't suggest improvements without first identifying weaknesses. If the two people involved in the feedback conversation have differing ideas about what they want to discuss, then the conversation will be doomed before it even starts. The first step is to be clear with the receiver about what you intend to provide and also ask what they are looking for. This doesn't have to be as stilted as 'Good day, sir/madam! I am going to have a coaching conversation with you. Are you willing and able to receive this conversation?' Start off just by talking. Ask how their lessons have gone and how their day has been, and you will quickly get an idea of where they are at mentally. This can allow you to tailor the feedback appropriately. If you and the receiver are far apart in your aims, you will need to align them towards yours or agree to feed back another time. There is no point wasting feedback on a person who is unwilling to hear it. You will, at best, make no change to their teaching or, at worst, lower their morale.

---

10 Self-report is a *Teach Like a Champion 2.0* technique whereby teachers are encouraged to not say things like 'everyone got it?' and instead ask specific questions which check that students have understood.

Triggers

Now that we have established the purpose of the feedback and we are aligned, we have the next hurdle to overcome: triggers. Triggers are barriers that prevent the feedback from being heard. The person might be receptive to feedback in general, but certain things about this particular piece of feedback might raise a barrier to listening. Stone and Heen identify three kinds of triggers that might stop a teacher listening to your feedback:[11]

1   **Relationship triggers:** The feedback might be spot on, but they don't respect your opinion so won't listen.

2   **Truth triggers:** The feedback just seems false from their point of view.

3   **Identity triggers:** The feedback makes them question something that they hold as part of their core persona. If the feedback is right, it will make them question who they really are.

All three triggers are common in teaching. School politics, policies and personalities make them inevitable. They are potentially there in any feedback conversation – an unavoidable obstacle that leaders need to navigate. It is in an observer's best interests to be wary of them when giving feedback, but the solution may not always be straightforward. For example, let's consider a simple relationship trigger. Imagine that as a new leader you are observing a staff member with whom you do not see eye to eye. You have disagreed in the past and your personalities tend to clash. This is your first time observing them as their superior and you have noticed some things that could be significantly improved.

This is not a situation that can be solved instantly. Well, you could solve the relationship issue by not telling the truth, lavishing appreciation on them, and avoiding confrontation. Unfortunately, this will not help the teacher or their students in the long run. If we agree that is not the way forward, then we can see that we need to have a candid conversation and use a few simple tips to ensure that some of the feedback is heard. Initially, this will not improve the relationship. However, if the feedback is specific and effective then as the teacher notices improvements in the classroom, they will recognise your good intentions and the relationship trigger will diminish.

As you can see, removing triggers is a complex issue with many context-dependent factors to consider. However, there are some general suggestions which will help:

● Make sure that your comments are detailed and considered, especially the positive ones. The detail shows that you care and avoids the risk of the listener brushing it away as a token gesture.

11 Stone and Heen, *Thanks for the Feedback.*

- If it is an issue that might seem hard to believe, find some proof. Might they agree to video a couple of lessons so that they can see for themselves? Or to have a second observer look at a different lesson? So many people have blind spots for certain aspects of their teaching.

- Present ideas for improvement as suggestions and then get them to commit to at least giving it a try and seeing how it goes. Instead of 'Use the visualiser to live model the paragraph', pose this as a question. 'Have you considered using the visualiser to live model the paragraph? Why not? Do you think we could put it down as something to try and see how it goes?' This removes the identity trigger as you are not threatening their key values (which in this case might be about the strength of their PowerPoints).

- Never underestimate the power of curiosity. Ask questions to direct the teacher towards the areas which you think they need to explore. 'You didn't check for understanding enough before the activity' becomes 'I'm curious, how many students do you think fully understood the instructions? How could we improve that number? One of the strategies that I've seen work well in other classes is …'

Feedback is a vital aspect of any learning walk system, but it is a tricky issue. Like most things in education, it is complex and not entirely under your control. As a leader, it is your duty to find a way to get the message through without destroying morale. After all, education is not a zero-sum game: we can all improve as teachers and as leaders, and we are all in it together.

Feedback mechanisms

Now that we know a lot more about how the structure of feedback affects its reception, the different ways of communicating it can be reviewed. As with all things a middle leader must deal with, there is a certain amount of pragmatism that needs to be applied. There are three main feedback mechanisms available to us:

1   **Written feedback:** Highly convenient for a busy middle leader. It's low-risk for appreciation and has the benefit of being recorded for posterity. However, it's high-risk for appraisal as you can't follow up with their responses to it and their feelings can't be influenced by the tone, to the extent that they can in a conversation. It does have the advantage of formality, which might be helpful, but is better as a follow-up to a conversation.

2 **Face-to-face feedback:** The best in terms of facilitating coaching and appraisal. It's great for appreciation too, but hugely time-consuming so needs to be used judiciously.

3 **Drive-by feedback:** Delivered when you just pop your head into a room or bump into someone in the corridor. It's hugely effective for appreciation, but catastrophic for appraisal and coaching because there is no time to actively check understanding and ensure that the messages are received as intended. Its convenience means that it is a tempting option, but it is best avoided. It will just waste your time and lower the recipient's morale.

Difficult conversations

One of the biggest mistakes of my leadership career occurred as a result of a coaching conversation. The coach and I were discussing the performance of a member of staff and some concerns about some Year 11 classes. The problem was that we had just come through a period of staffing crisis and so my approach to ensuring that my staff were happy was to fiercely defend them to the SLT and become more accepting of poor teaching. During a coaching conversation we discussed whether there was time for the staff member to improve or if I needed to rewrite the timetable to ensure that those Year 11s were not adversely affected. We also discussed whether it was better to be honest with the teacher and tell them the reason or to lie and protect their feelings. We settled on the truth as it was the only way they could improve, and we owed it to them to be honest. Also, as this was due to student-driven complaints, there was a risk that the students would bring it to their attention if we didn't.

A couple of days later I met the teacher and laid it all out. I used Andy Buck's NEFI ART structure to ensure that I carried out the conversation in a professional way.[12]

NEFI ART

Name: Name the issue.

Example: Give a specific example.

Feelings: Describe how you feel about the situation.

Important: Explain why it matters so much.

---

12 A. Buck, Difficult Conversations, *Buck's Fizz* [blog] (1 August 2018). Available at: https://andybuckblog.wordpress.com/2018/08/01/difficult-conversations/.

> **Accept:** Accept your role in the problem.
>
> **Resolve:** Show you want to resolve the issue.
>
> **Them:** Invite them to respond.

I did the best job I could to reassure the teacher that I would be working closely with them and supporting them in this temporary setback, but that changes had to be made. It did not go well. What followed was a term and a half of severe absence and then, in the summer, they moved to a different school. Also, they developed severe animosity towards me. I found this difficult to deal with because at the time I saw myself very much as a leader who worked for my team first, then the students.

For a long time, I was angry about the coaching session. I was sure that if only I had followed my instincts, I could have sold them the lie and fixed their performance slowly through incremental coaching. Now, with the benefit of hindsight and greater self-understanding, I realise that the coaching session gave rise to the right decision. The problem was that I had created a department culture in which I ignored issues to boost morale. This created a challenge when I was finally forced to deal with an issue that had grown from a minor classroom practice matter to a major concern. Because I wasn't candid early on, the teacher went from thinking that they were performing perfectly well to having their identity as a teacher severely challenged in one observation. In short, I had created an environment in which molehills had grown into mountains and now staff were paying the price.

NEFI ART is a great system for difficult conversations, but it is not magic. When it comes to challenging conversations, any system will not work unless the culture you create in your team is appropriate. Again, this epiphany came when I read Kim Scott's book *Radical Candor*. In it she makes a compelling case for the need to create frequent open dialogues around feedback. Her 2019 revised edition's introduction laments how often her idea is interpreted as a green light to just be blunt and horrible.[13] However, this is not the case. Used correctly, radical candour is an incredibly powerful tool for building a team that is open and honest with each other. To get a team to embrace candid conversations, it all starts with you. You must go out of your way to receive feedback and take it on the chin. Even if it triggers you, you need to be thankful for it and avoid instantly discrediting it. This way you can model the fact that it is OK to receive feedback. Remember, feedback is a gift.

---

13 K. Scott, *Radical Candor: How to Get What You Want by Saying What You Mean*, revised edn (London: Pan Macmillan, 2019).

Being candid requires strong relationships with your team and genuine care. You need to know what each other's motives are, and they need to know that you are committed to helping them be the best they can be. This doesn't mean that you have to spend time outside of work or become close friends with all of them, but if they ask themselves whether you have their best interests at heart, the answer has to be a resounding 'yes'. This trust is going to be vital. It means moving at their pace and putting in the time required to help them secure the success they deserve. Basically, being a decent human being.

Challenge directly, which is not saying 'be blunt with the truth' or worse 'be obnoxious in the guise of being a straight shooter'. Challenging directly is about being honest and assertive in a way that shows you care. You care so much about their professional development that you want to help them reach their potential. The old adage 'coaches only shout at players with potential' comes to mind. Although please don't shout. If something could be better, then people need to know as early as possible so they can be supported. Feedback that is wishy-washy tends to be ignored.

If we can show that we care personally and challenge directly, it allows team members to become aware of their strengths and weaknesses. If they can know that they can communicate any issues back to you then you will begin to understand your team much better. The ability to speak truth to power makes them more receptive to receiving feedback without triggering any barriers.

We are encouraged to use a similar dynamic with our students: we aim to be warm but strict with them. With our team, we aim to be candid but compassionate.

Recap

- Leading others is a privilege but also a huge responsibility.

- Using leadership surveys to identify your leadership personality will not unlock some hidden potential and solve all your problems.

- Teams are unique and have their own eccentricities. Get to know your team and what makes them tick.

- Leading well takes authenticity and involves walking the walk. This is incredibly hard.

- The elephant, rider and the path is a great tool for finding ways to introduce change without reducing morale.

- As well as managing your team, you need to manage your line manager. Managing up is all about identifying your line manager's strengths and limitations. Once identified, you can adapt your approach to get the most from the partnership.

- Feedback is often hard to hear and people are resistant to ideas which do not fit with their expectations of the conversation. These triggers can be overcome by being clear about the intended purpose at the start.

- Care personally about your team to build rapport, but don't be afraid to challenge things that need to change. This doesn't mean being horrible; it does mean being honest.

Reflect

- Do I know my team? What are their predispositions?

- Who are my superstars and rockstars?

- How do I normally manage change? Do I consider the elephant, the rider and the path?

- What are my line manager's key motives? Am I doing all I can to create an effective two-way relationship?

- Do I have a team that can embrace candid conversations in a non-hostile way? If not, what is the first step to making that happen?

- Think back to the last time you received feedback. Were there any triggers in it? Were you both clear about its purpose?

- Think back to the last time you gave feedback. Did you manage to make the purpose clear and avoid triggers?

Chapter 9
Wellbeing

Canst thou, O partial sleep, give thy repose

To the wet sea-boy in an hour so rude;

And in the calmest and most stillest night,

With all appliances and means to boot,

Deny it to a king? Then, happy low, lie down!

Uneasy lies the head that wears a crown.

King Henry[1]

A few years ago, I vividly recall logging into my mortgage account and feverishly tapping away on a calculator to figure out how I could keep paying my mortgage if I resigned my post as head of department. I had reached my limit. The pressure of the role was immense, and I was feeling the weight of expectations from leadership, my desire to protect my staff and my moral obligation to the students. I had been head of department for about 18 months and things were not going great. I was at a loss as to how to turn around the department and in pure panic mode. This is not to say that my school was toxic. In fact, it was improving in terms of its expectations on staff and its use of evidence. We had some staffing gaps, which lead to a carousel of supply teachers and its associated issues. The whole situation led to me having a huge sense of outrage. Why was I in this position? Didn't they know how hard I was working? It's not my fault!

I had to make a choice. I knew I couldn't go on this way and I realised three things:

1   I needed to take a step back and come up with a strategy that I could follow.

2   I needed to find a way of changing my own reaction to the situation.

3   I needed to overcome my total lack of ideas about how to proceed.

This chapter starts at this point in my life and discusses some of the most important things that helped me move forward. It then takes these themes and expands them into actionable techniques that can be used to support others. I suppose that makes this

---

1   W. Shakespeare, *Henry IV Part 2*, Act 3, Scene 1.

chapter a bit more subjective, in a way, but I hope you can see how these ideas might be applied to your situation. It was at this point that I began my journey into Twitter and blogging. Through the connections I made I came across the work of Austrian psychotherapist Alfred Adler.[2] I believe Adler's interpretation of human psychology is incredibly appropriate for teachers. Teaching is very much a job that can expand to fill your whole life and encourage you to believe that you have more control than you really do. For leaders, this feeling can be magnified. Adlerian psychology really helped me to see the boundaries of my job more clearly and that has massively reduced my stress levels. I want to outline some of the more pertinent aspects of his ideas here. *The Courage to Be Disliked* by Ichiro Kishimi and Fumitake Koga is an excellent examination of these ideas and more.[3] If you find this chapter useful, I would recommend reading it.

One of the more unique aspects of teaching that can contribute to stress and weaken mental health is the relationship between the accountability placed on teachers and the way in which their impact is measured. Teachers are often held accountable for their students' outcomes. On the surface this makes sense, but once you start to consider all the aspects that lead to a singular outcome of an examination result – like the student, the school culture and parental involvement, for example – it becomes obvious that teachers play an important, but minor, role in outcomes. That doesn't mean that we shouldn't aim to maximise the impact of teaching, just that by placing a teacher's worth entirely on examination results we are magnifying the pressure on teachers. There is another form of accountability, however: the moral accountability that teachers put upon themselves. This is a strong motivator and, for some, stronger than any external judgement.

I've never met a teacher who doesn't care about the students they teach. I have met teachers who dislike their students and the job, but that often stemmed from frustration built up over years of being powerless to prevent students making all too predictably poor decisions about their education. I've also met teachers who feel besieged. They have been told that they are not teaching to the required standard and given high levels of support and scrutiny. They have grown to resent the profession and have built a wall around themselves. They don't engage in professional learning, and feedback and advice are perceived as threats. They didn't start out this way, but it's the coping mechanism that they have adopted to survive. We discussed these issues in Chapter 5. For these reasons, and countless others, some teachers struggle massively with their mental health each year.

---

2   A. Adler, *Understanding Life: An Introduction to the Psychology of Alfred Adler*, tr. C. Brett (Oxford: Oneworld, 2009).

3   I. Kishimi and F. Koga, *The Courage to Be Disliked: How to Free Yourself, Change Your Life and Achieve Real Happiness* (Sydney: Allen & Unwin, 2013).

Adlerian psychology

Alfred Adler was an Austrian medical doctor who began to explore the concepts of psychoanalysis at the same time as Freud. He was also a member of the famous Vienna Psychoanalytic Society. Adlerian psychology differs hugely from Freudian psychoanalysis. I think it is the seed of many pragmatic, solution-focused therapeutic approaches like CBT. It also closely aligns with the philosophy of stoicism – so if you are familiar with these areas, some of the ideas might not be new.

Aetiology vs teleology

Aetiology: The study of causation.

Teleology: The study of the purpose of a given phenomenon.

The most powerful aspect of Adlerian psychology is that it is teleological in its nature. Instead of taking an aetiological perspective, like so many therapeutic approaches, Adlerian psychology takes a teleological one. It chooses not to focus on the *traumas* of the past, or the *causes* of these, but instead its focus lies squarely on the *meaning attributed* to past events.

This is one of the main pillars of Adlerian psychology. When applied to working in a school, it makes total sense. So many of the things that affect a teacher day-to-day are out of their control: policies they don't agree with, students' attitudes and, famously, the weather, to take a few examples. This can lead to negative thoughts and a feeling of helplessness that can manifest as anxiety. The events of last year, last week or even last lesson are not really relevant when thinking teleologically; we choose to think about the here and now. Teleological thinking forces us to consider the *meaning* we give current and past events. By placing the focus on actions in the here and now, we focus on ways to change our outlook, instead of putting our energies into trying to move immovable objects.

Trauma does not exist

If you have dealt with any child protection issues, you will no doubt know that trauma does not inform behaviour in *all* cases. In every school there are students who have case-files filled with horrific incidents but who present as perfectly 'normal' children or teenagers. Likewise, some of the most high-profile students in your school will come from very mundane situations with no apparent 'reason' to behave in the way they do. Adlerian psychology rejects the idea that trauma *causes* certain behaviours, because that would be an aetiological approach. This is seen as controversial as there is a body of evidence, and associated strategies, about becoming *trauma-informed* in our practice. Adlerian psychology is not saying that traumatic events do not affect a person's life; rather, it simply maintains that we can't change what happened in the past. Teleological approaches look at the meaning we attribute to the events in our lives. This means that we are, in fact, not victims of circumstance but narrators of our own past, using events to tell our life stories to suit our own agenda.

Let's consider a fictitious, and fairly benign, example to illustrate this point. Let's say I'm sitting outside a cafe and you walk past. I raise my hand and wave, calling out 'Hi'. You do not respond and walk right past me. The effect the incident has on my mental health is completely down to how much meaning I put into it. If I choose to take it as a sign that you have snubbed me, then I can use the incident to create a sense of hostility, paranoia and even a shame spiral. I can let it affect both my self-worth and my perception of our relationship. Or I can choose to see it as one of those things that happens sometimes. There are many reasons why you might not have responded – perhaps you did not hear me or were distracted. In teleology the incident is benign; the subjective view you take has the power. Most importantly, *you* are responsible for the power and impact it has on your life. You are in control.

I often think the biggest mistake a teacher can make is getting sucked into the idea that a class' behaviour is a reflection on their professional quality. I know a lot of teachers who take an aetiological view in these situations – both in judging themselves and, unfortunately, in judging others. If they have a bad lesson with a tough class, they infer that they are a weak teacher. They are embarrassed and wish to avoid observation. Never is this more common than with trainee teachers. Teleology tells us instead to consider how much meaning we attribute to *that* class. Can we see that poor behaviour is a result of a multitude of factors? Can we remember that a teacher's quality shouldn't be determined by looking at just one class? Can we avoid going home with a black cloud above us and steeping ourselves in feelings of failure and incompetence? By keeping that one class in perspective, we make ourselves more open to support from observation and increase our chances of improving the class' behaviour by allowing outside support in without fear of ruining our reputation.

Anger

Once, many years ago, I was teaching a top set. I had them round the front desk and I was about to demonstrate something. I had asked for silence a couple of times, but some boys were still talking. I had known them since they were 7 years old. I had been their basketball coach, taking them to matches around the county. I knew their families well and they knew mine. After a few moments of waiting I achieved silence. As I began to discuss the apparatus, the boys began talking again. I completely lost it. I screamed at them and, like a stroppy toddler, threw my register folder (see, told you it was a long time ago) across the room. The folder hit the wall with a crash. Silence fell on the class. Everyone rightly looked at me like I was losing it. I apologised, picked up the now bent ring binder and returned to the lesson. My pulse was up and I was sweating as the adrenaline subsided. For many years I wondered why I got so angry. Adlerian psychology offers an unusual, but powerful, explanation: people fabricate anger.

Consider the situation of a noisy class that is ignoring a teacher's instructions. Some teachers will get angry, some will shout, shame the students, or get aggressive, like I did. Others will use a calm tone and strategies like sanctions. All teachers will feel frustrated in that situation, but how they react is based on the *meaning* they give to that frustration. I'm not saying that the teacher who gets angry is wrong, but that a teacher *decides* – at some level – to get angry because it suits their goal and provides an approach to achieve their aims. Adlerian psychology says that anger is a tool used to justify the strategy you wish to use. In short, you didn't shout at the class because you got angry, you got angry because you wanted to shout at the class. Why did you want to shout at the class? I'm not sure – possibly because you wanted them to submit to your will as quickly as possible? Maybe you wanted to let off some frustration, so you don't have to keep hold of it through the day? Only you can answer that question.

In my case, I think it was a way to make the students submit to my power; it was designed to scare them from crossing me again and intimidate them into behaving better in the future. I had taken their behaviour personally, and I wanted them to feel as upset as I was. I felt that while they might not behave for other teachers, they *should* behave for me because I had built up a strong relationship with them outside of the classroom. I know better now.

The fabrication of anger is one of the harder messages that Adler has for us. Most people live with the idea that anger causes us to behave in uncontrollable ways, but this is simply not true. To illustrate this point, consider how you would react to a misbehaving class if you had a knife in your hand. If anger were truly an uncontrollable rage, in that situation you would have started threatening students with the knife. However, I'm sure that you would definitely not behave in that way under any circumstance. Therefore, if there is an upper limit to the acceptable behaviour, there must be a choice made, even if it is only unconscious. I realise that this is a somewhat contrived analogy, but the essence of the conclusion is what is important.

All emotional problems are interpersonal relationship problems

Adler's view was that humans are essentially social animals and that all our emotional issues rise out of problems with interpersonal relationships. I'm sure that – as with any generalisation – there might be exceptions that instantly spring to your mind. However, my experience has been that, if carefully and honestly evaluated in most situations, the reason for the emotional distress is to do with an interpersonal relationship issue. I'll try to illustrate this with a few examples:

- You get upset when a senior teacher comes into your classroom and the class is unfocused.

- You receive a letter from a parent complaining about a student's poor test result.

- You stay behind to help run revision sessions and your line manager does not thank you or show appreciation of your efforts.

- A student swears at you and refuses to follow your instructions.

- An exams officer lets a student sit the wrong tier of mock exam.

In these situations, how you feel will be more about your interpersonal relationships than anything else. If you feel secure in the other's opinion of you, you will be able to cope relatively well in these instances. If you have a fractious relationship, then these events could cause great anxiety. The uncomfortable truth is that all emotional issues are, when distilled down, about interpersonal relationships. If we are aware of the status of a relationship, and accepting of it, it can allow us to understand why we have strong reactions in certain situations. We can acknowledge our emotions and their causes, and try to look beyond them as we recognise that we are not an impartial narrator of this event.

Goals and lifestyle

As mentioned previously, the behaviour displayed by a person is chosen to achieve a goal. It may be that the individual will find it incredibly hard to admit the goal, but the goal nonetheless remains. Think back to an emotive event that happened last term – think about your reactions and emotions. What was your goal? Try to identify the goal of your emotion. Were you trying to get someone to see your point of view? Or bow to your will? Or were you just after sympathy? Were you trying to gain power or get them to solve your problem for you?

The goals you set yourself are linked to your *lifestyle*. Adlerian psychology attributes a broader meaning to this word than just diet, consumer choices, economic status, etc., to include your personality and various cultural influences. The challenge, if you choose to accept it, is to acknowledge that you have chosen your lifestyle to achieve your goals. This can make you feel really terrible if you are not happy, as it means that it's no one's fault but yours – and that is tough to swallow. You may not have consciously realised it but events and, more importantly, the meaning you attributed to them have formed a lifestyle that affirms your goals.

So let's say a fictitious person, Xander, is an unhappy middle leader. He is struggling to get to work and has lost his joy for the job. He is under large amounts of pressure from line management due to student outcomes, and a couple of learning walks have identified concerns, including about one of his own lessons. On the surface it might seem that all these things are bound to make someone unhappy and that they are all out of Xander's control. On closer inspection, how Xander feels about these things depends on his lifestyle. If his goals are to prove that his line manager is out to get him, that no one understands him and that it's not fair, then he can use this situation to make himself the victim and maligned party. If his goal is to find joy in the job again, and improve his teaching and that of the team, then he can take the situation as an opportunity for growth. He can embrace support, learn from others, and hopefully improve his teaching. I fully understand that how these events unfold is also a huge factor in how easy it is to choose one interpretation over the other, but it is still a choice being made. As leaders, this should not give us carte blanche to treat team members badly and blame them for their reactions; rather, it should give us pause for thought about how we react in situations and also how people sometimes react to us.

What can we change when we can't change the school?

To a classroom teacher the inability to create change is a key cause of stress and anxiety. Often, they are powerless to make changes that they feel passionately about. This leads to a feeling of injustice and resentment. This can also happen to middle leaders. Changes might feel 'done unto' them, and the motives behind the change might seem to be more to do with senior leaders' personal agendas than actually solving problems. This is a highly subjective judgement and is hugely affected by the amount of information the teacher or middle leader has. Decisions at the senior leadership level are affected by many factors of which the classroom teacher or middle leader is unaware. A classroom teacher has very little influence on those kinds of decisions. As a middle leader you can't change your school, but you can change your area of responsibility. As we discussed in Chapter 6, you should consider all decisions based on how they affect classroom teachers. While you are not personally responsible for your team's wellbeing, you are responsible for creating a climate which aims to improve it.

Staff wellbeing

Leaders are very aware that staff wellbeing is a vital part of creating a successful school. Schools try to improve wellbeing by promoting activities like yoga, mindfulness and cake eating. However, none of these initiatives really improve a teacher's wellbeing. At best they say, 'We know it's a hard job and we appreciate you sticking at it.' Don't get me wrong, appreciation matters, but it pales in comparison to other mechanisms of evaluation – such as performance management, marking practices and various internal quality-assurance policies. As mentioned previously, we can't always change our situation, but we can change our outlook on it. What we need is a change of perspective.

The separation of tasks

Adlerian psychology defines this change in outlook as the *separation of tasks*. Tasks are essentially the roles we play. Stated simply, when we come across something that is causing us difficulty, we need to ask ourselves 'What are my tasks and what are other people's tasks?' An example that often comes up in middle leadership is to do with in-year performance data. During the year teachers are asked to report this, often generating predicted grades. The teacher's task is to report class data based on predetermined criteria, not to consider the implications of that data. As soon as the teacher begins to think about the percentage of students 'on target' they will subconsciously make their students' reports more positive, which is an example of anchoring. By doing so they fail to perform the initial task correctly. It is the middle leader's task to consider the overall outcome, the reliability of the data and next steps, not the teacher's.

Another classic example comes from lesson observations. High-stakes lesson observations and tick lists of expectations can create a climate in which the task of the teacher changes from educating the students as well as possible to impressing the observer with strategies A, B or C. Their task is not 'be the best teacher possible', but instead 'be perceived as a good teacher in the observer's eyes'. This is understandable as reputation is hugely important, both for progression and for ensuring that they have the space to develop their own practice as they see fit. In an ideal world those two tasks would be one and the same, but I know from reading Twitter that ideas about what great teaching looks like vary massively. Over the years this also evolves. Chapter 5 reminded us of the value of principles over practices, and I think this is one way to ensure that we allow teachers to focus on the important tasks.

As leaders we often have to deal with team members' underperformance. If a senior colleague draws attention to an issue with a teacher not following a procedure or using a recommended strategy, our initial reaction could be one of anger or frustration with the team member. They have not followed our instructions and they have let the side down! Let's consider this scenario from a non-Adlerian and an Adlerian approach. This way we can see how the tools can work together to support us.

Non-Adlerian

We start with frustration. 'Why didn't they get it right? I made it so simple!' Next comes the fear and embarrassment that it reflects on the colleague's opinion of you as a leader. 'What if they tell the rest of the SLT?' The emotions turn to anger. 'If they couldn't be bothered to do this for me then they must not believe in me as a leader. I said it was important! I bet they never agreed with my idea anyway and thought they'd just ignore me.' The stress and anger bubble over and when you finally talk to the team member your sentences are short and it is clear that you are annoyed. They give you a reason, but you are too angry to accept it and you leave on the simple command, 'Get it right next time, please.'

Adlerian

We start with frustration. 'Why didn't they get it right? I made it so simple!' Next comes the fear and embarrassment that it reflects on the colleague's opinion of you as a leader.

Crucially, at this point you undergo the separation of tasks. You recognise that you gave clear instructions and that it is not your task to make them do it; that is their task. You just have to ensure that they know what, why and how. You also might acknowledge your role in reminding them. This means that your embarrassment wanes and you choose not to be angry. You don't see it as a value judgement on your leadership and you approach the team member with curiosity – you seek to understand what happened. When hearing the team member's reasoning, you do not believe that it is acceptable. You challenge them about the importance of the task and discuss how they will ensure that they perform it. You leave on the simple request, 'Get it right next time, please.'

The following questions are for you to reflect on your emotional resilience:

- How much power do you give past events in determining your mood today?

- How much energy do you invest in things that you have no control over?

- Do you find it easy to identify the reasons why you decided to become a teacher or leader?

- When you get angry, what is your goal? Is there a better way of achieving that goal?

- If you are faced with an emotionally difficult situation that is making you anxious, look to the interpersonal relationships involved. Is there a cause for anxiety there? What could you do to change those relationships and reduce the anxiety? If you can't change the relationships, can you change the way in which you view them?

- When considering your response to a challenging situation, carefully consider your goals. Be honest with yourself. What are you trying to achieve? Does your lifestyle honestly reflect the goals you think you have?

- When facing a difficult situation, complete the separation of tasks and consider how you will focus on your tasks. What will you do to remind yourself that some things are not your tasks?

How to avoid friendly fire: creating buffers

With the best will in the world there are going to be times when even the most resilient minds feel strained by the role of middle leadership. A school day as a middle leader is a hectic cacophony of lessons, duties, crisis management and high-stakes decision making. On top of that there are the meetings or vital jobs that need to be completed after students leave, and the desire to get home at a vaguely reasonable time. When I first became head of department, my own two children were young, so I always wanted to get home for 5 p.m. so I could help with dinner and support my wife. I would zoom through my pointless marking and vital planning, rush to the photocopier to ensure that I was ready for the next day and then jump on my bike to make the short journey home. I'd rush through the door and start helping straight away – with a scowl on my face and short temper. My wife would put the radio on while we cooked and I found the background noise unbearable. I would be unable to concentrate and have an urge to turn it off and ask for silence like I was entering a Year 9 cover lesson. This caused friction and resentment at home and the odd argument.

Fortunately, I received a piece of sage advice from a colleague. He told me to find five minutes to create a buffer between school and home. So, once I had finished work, I would cycle home but stop on the way and just let my frustrations from the day go. I'm lucky in that I can cycle past the beach, which is a perfect location. When the weather was bad, I would just move to a corner of my classroom and try to switch off and decompress a little. As my wise friend told me, 'Being five minutes late is not a big deal but being horrible to your family is.' If you commute and don't get more riled up by traffic, perhaps the drive can provide this. Personally, I hate traffic and would still need at least a minute to compose myself when I got home. Buffers help us to avoid cross-contamination between work and home. This can work both ways, as sometimes home can be a source of stress at certain times of people's lives.

Work–life balance: not a one-size-fits-all approach

It is strange how people are so prone to projecting their values onto everyone else. There is more than one way to get things done, but we are quick to draw conclusions if someone else is doing things differently. This is clear in the debate among school leaders about work–life balance and wellbeing. I have read and heard quite a few leaders pontificating about wellbeing. Loads brag about how they have blanket policies that mean emails can't be sent or received between 6 p.m. and 7 a.m. They often follow this with some triumphant decree like 'Our school takes wellbeing seriously; people need a work–life balance.'[4]

I have a big problem with this, though. You see, by not getting emails in the evening and early morning, it doesn't mean that I will have fewer emails, so it doesn't actually affect my workload. It just means I have less time to answer my emails. It's the same with people who chime in when they see you on your phone: 'Oh, I could never have my work emails

---

4   If you are imagining the voice of Lucius Malfoy here, then you and I are in sync and I applaud you.

on my phone, such a degradation of my work–life balance!'[5] They are ignoring the fact that by doing this I can actually solve problems as they arise. This means that when I get into school, I don't have 50 things to do and can actually check on my team. I know a couple of incredibly productive working mothers who swear by their phone as a way of maximising their effectiveness during the day and gaining free time to spend with their children. When considering wellbeing, please keep an open mind. What works for one might not work for all, and blanket policies might be doing more harm than good. Please don't feel guilty if you have your work emails on your phone. You are not a workaholic; you just prefer to work on demand. After all, you can always put your phone on silent or minimise notifications. Similarly, if having work emails on your phone makes you anxious and stressed, just don't! It's all about working out what fits best with your lifestyle. The job has to work for you, or it will slowly eat you up. The best approach is to lead by example. If it's late and it suits your way of working, hold non-urgent emails back and send them the following day. Or, if you must send them, make it explicit in the email that you do not expect a reply until the next working day. Just avoid the sanctimonious approach that implies you know what is best for everyone and I'm sure your team will appreciate it.

The wellbeing of your team: what does and doesn't matter

Schools really struggle to get wellbeing right. When talking about wellbeing I think it is really important to keep in mind Hanlon's razor: 'Never attribute to malice that which is adequately explained by stupidity.'[6] I've heard people discuss their experiences of toxic school environments and situations. They always describe the leader as some sort of Bond villain, hell-bent on making them work through the night. This is nonsense. The leader in question is probably just completely clueless and a bit selfish. They are thinking of things from their own perspective and when they try to imagine what school life is like for a classroom teacher they are so far removed that the rose-tinted glasses of egocentric bias mean that they think they would have easily been able to achieve all the tasks prescribed in the time provided. One of the worst wellbeing gifts I ever received was a bottle of wine. It came with a tag which read 'Thanks for all your hard work this term'.

This was a problem for two reasons. The first was superficial – I don't drink wine – but secondly, and more importantly, half of that hard work was created by the person who had given me the wine. This would have been fine if the work was meaningful, but quite frankly it was box-ticking admin, with which I, and a lot of the team, did not agree.

5 For the record this should be read in the voice of Samantha from *Sex and the City*.
6 See https://quoteinvestigator.com/2016/12/30/not-malice/.

Wellbeing is not Cadbury's Creme Egg at Easter. It is not yoga straight after school on a Wednesday; I can't go without taking along the 60 books I need to mark later that night! Wellbeing comes from showing that you care and listening to how systems are impacting staff. Wellbeing is not a popularity contest to see who can make staff the happiest, because we need to maintain effectiveness for our students. Review your policies, starting with marking. Look at the evidence and research on effective strategies and prioritise those that will reduce workload. Get the team to contribute their thoughts and listen to others'. Once you have a culture of trust and have shown that you care about staff wellbeing, all the tokenistic strategies – like selection boxes at Christmas and staff awards – will have a massive value because they will be a sign of appreciation instead of an apology.

Here is a list of some great wellbeing strategies:

- Give the department autonomy to set their own feedback policy.
- Move from marking to feedback, and recognise the variety of effective strategies.
- Implement a whole-school detention system, staffed by leaders.
- Implement a whole-school behaviour system which does not undermine teachers.
- Reduce the number of meetings so you only have the essential ones.

Notice how the capital cost of these initiatives is very small. It's not about money; it's about the culture. However, getting these concessions can be difficult. You might have to fight uphill to get the flexibility to improve your staff wellbeing. Some of the biggies are out of your control. But if you are organised and have done your research then it's a battle worth having. I've always found that the best argument is along the lines of the classic: 'If you don't look after your customers then someone else will.' Plenty of schools with wellbeing embedded are more than willing to take your best staff – that often gets senior leaders' attention.

Helping a member of staff in crisis

Let's say you walk into the staffroom and you see a member of your team in tears. There is a small crowd huddled around them and five minutes until the next lesson. The mantle of leadership often requires you to go outside of your job specification to support those you lead. But how best do you offer support in these situations? Staff can go into crisis mode for many reasons: it could be a bereavement, tragic news about a loved one's health, or even an incident at school. The reason is less important than the effect it has on them. For our purposes, we are going to ignore the reason and focus on the fact that they are so upset they are unable to teach next lesson and need support right now.

Below is an outline of things I have learnt from experience and also advice from Kevin Robbins, a school counsellor with over 20 years' experience helping staff and students in crisis.[7] We will also draw on some advice from bereavement research. This is not a panacea and is not to be followed as a step-by-step guide, but I have attempted to structure this advice in chronological order. In the moment you will forget some things, and you can't really practise your response, so don't worry – just do your best.

You never know when you are going to find someone in crisis, so it is best to be prepared. As a good tip it is always worth having a pack of tissues in your bag/classroom. They will be needed.

Upon discovering the distressed staff member:

- Acknowledge them. So often people get so caught up in thinking about what to do next that they forget to actually acknowledge the person in distress. Tell them you want to help and will be back in a minute once you've sorted everything out.

- If there is a crowd, ask one member of staff to stay with them. Give the rest of them jobs to do from further down this list. It keeps them useful and buys some privacy.

- Get cover: for them and for you. Supporting them probably won't take all lesson, but you need to make time in case it is needed.

- Find a private, comfortable space. If you have an office or an empty room, use it – you need to be somewhere you can talk without interruption for about 30 minutes.

- Don't forget the tissues.

During the conversation:

- Make the aim clear. 'Have a seat. We've got 30 minutes to talk. What's happened?'

- Now you need to actively listen. Shut down that internal voice in your head and just listen. Stop trying to solve their problem and just listen. There will be time for all the other stuff later, so just listen. Be empathetic, not sympathetic. Work hard to hear what is really being said. Be interested in them, not in your connection with what they are saying. This is not a conversation; you are listening to them.

- If the person is struggling to speak, don't be afraid to just wait. If this persists for a few minutes, you can start by asking, 'What would help you in this difficult time?'

---

7   Yes, he is my father.

- Be interested in the subject. 'What was the dog's name?' 'How long did she have cancer?' 'What was your father like?' 'How did it all start?'

- Keep listening. If you must ask questions to clarify facts, then try to keep them open.

- Sometimes the topic can hit a raw nerve related to your own life. Don't be afraid of your own feelings, but do remember that your stuff should be held back and worked through afterwards.

- Don't get scared because you think you can't cope with what you might hear. You can.

- Table 8 contains dos and don'ts for these situations, so bear these in mind.

After the conversation:

- Follow up. Make sure you keep relevant people in the loop. Will this have knock-on effects for the team? Are there questions to which you need answers?

- Follow through. Get in touch later on or the following day. A simple email or text will do – just let them know that you care.

Table 8: Some dos and don'ts for helping staff in crisis

Do	Don't
Do show you care.	Don't let your own sense of helplessness stop you reaching out.
Do be available – to listen, to run errands, or to do whatever else seems needed.	Don't avoid them because you are uncomfortable. This only adds to their pain.
Do say you are sorry about what happened and about their pain.	Don't say you know how they feel.

Do	Don't
Do allow them to express feelings as they experience them if they choose to.	Don't say, 'You ought to be feeling better by now', or anything else that judges their feelings.
Do encourage them to be patient with themselves and not impose any 'shoulds'.	Don't tell them what they should feel.
Do allow them to talk about the issue as much and as often as they want to.	Don't change the subject when they mention the issue. Don't avoid mentioning the people involved out of fear of reminding them of their pain. They haven't forgotten it.
Do reassure them that they did everything they could at the time.	Don't try to find something positive from the event.

Our final chapter has been all about wellbeing. We've looked at ways to support ourselves and our teams. I'm conscious that you might not agree with everything in this chapter, but I have no way of taking into account your viewpoint and experiences. Please don't take offence if I have said anything with which you completely disagree. These issues can be very emotive, and I do recognise that.

Recap

- Adlerian psychology can provide a framework to help us develop our emotional resilience.
- Teleology is a powerful tool. It gives us the ability to find ways to exercise control.
- Anger is a choice that occurs for a purpose. Acknowledging that helps us to maintain an even keel.

- All emotional problems are interpersonal relationship problems. If you find yourself having a strong emotional reaction to an event/issue, consider analysing your relationship with the person involved to understand why and allow you to move on.

- Work–life balance looks different to different individuals. Try not to impose your preferences on your team.

- Buffers are a way of preventing emotional cross-contamination between home and school.

- Staff wellbeing is rooted in systems, not tokens. Once the culture and systems are right, the gestures will be valued.

- Middle leaders occasionally need to support a team member in crisis. Having some strategies in mind before you first need to do so, and following some simple tips, can make the situation less challenging – and you more supportive.

Reflect

- How do I feel about Adlerian psychology? Could it help me to change my reaction to certain situations?

- What are my tasks? What are other people's tasks? Do I need to ask anyone to check that I know the limits of my role and responsibility?

- How do I use anger (in the classroom and outside of it)?

- If I have areas that cause me anxiety, have I considered the role of my interpersonal relationships with those involved?

- What is my buffer? Is it sustainable and complementary to my personal life?

- How do my policies affect the wellbeing of my team? Are there any areas that could be improved without affecting performance?

- If I reflect on a time a staff member was in crisis, how well did I do? Did I remember to listen? What would I do differently next time?

Conclusion

Middle leadership is an incredibly challenging job. In this book I've tried to provide a wide range of ideas to support you in developing your ability to lead your team. Hopefully you have found the chapters useful. I hope that I have challenged some of your preconceptions about what matters in leadership and given you some new strategies that you can deploy. I also want to make it clear that, while I have anointed myself as an expert in middle leadership, I am by no means a perfect leader. If, while reading, you thought to yourself, 'How on earth does he manage to do all this?' Well the answer is simple: I don't. Not all the time anyway. The job is hard and the aim is to do as much of the good stuff and as little of the bad as possible.

In all leadership, context is so important. While I am prone to writing with an air of self-importance, please remember that I fully accept that there is more than one way to lead a team. Each school is different and therefore each team is different. A leader's job is to understand their own context in as much detail as possible, accrue as many potential solutions as possible and have the wisdom to make the right call. Then it is just the simple task of communicating that plan, overcoming any logistical barriers and delivering the change without losing the team. When you look at it that way, it's quite miraculous we ever get it to work! Oh, and don't forget the quality assurance and evaluation of impact that comes later down the line. If you are currently a middle leader in a school then I applaud you; if you are someone looking to move into leadership then I encourage you. Middle leaders are the people who drive a school forward and your staff and students appreciate the work you do, although they might never tell you. Thanks for reading.

Bibliography

Adler, A. (2009). *Understanding Life: An Introduction to the Psychology of Alfred Adler*, tr. C. Brett (Oxford: Oneworld).

Allen, B. (2018). What If We Cannot Measure Pupil Progress? *Becky Allen: Musings on Education Policy* [blog] (23 May). Available at: https://rebeccaallen.co.uk/2018/05/23/what-if-we-cannot-measure-pupil-progress/.

Allison, S. (2016). Subject Planning and Development Sessions, *Class Teaching* [blog] (19 September). Available at: https://classteaching.wordpress.com/2016/09/19/subject-planning-and-development-sessions/.

Ashbee, R. (2019). The 10 Features of Highly Effective Curriculum Planning, *Reflections in Science Education* [blog] (11 February). Available at: https://reflectionsinscience.wordpress.com/2019/02/11/the-10-features-of-highly-effective-curriculum-planning-a-guest-blog/.

Ashbee, R. (2020). Vertical, Horizontal, Hierarchical, Cumulative, Integrative, Discursive, *The Fruits Are Sweet* [blog] (11 February). Available at: https://rosalindwalker.wordpress.com/2020/02/11/vertical-horizontal-hierarchical-cumulative-integrative-discursive/.

Atkinson, R. C. and R. M. Shiffrin (1968). Human Memory: A Proposed System and Its Control Processes. In K. W. Spence and J. T. Spence (eds), *The Psychology of Learning and Motivation, Volume 2* (New York: Academic Press), pp. 89–195.

Baddeley, A. D. and G. J. Hitch (1974). Working Memory. In G. A. Bower (ed.), *Recent Advances in Learning and Motivation, Volume 8* (New York: Academic Press), pp. 47–89.

Baker, C. (2020). We Need to Talk About E-mail and Meetings: Planning Your School's Internal Communication, *Medium* [blog] (14 May). Available at: https://medium.com/@chrisbakerphysics/we-need-to-talk-about-e-mail-and-meetings-planning-your-schools-internal-communication-db1257ce91de.

Bambrick-Santoyo, P. (2016). *Get Better Faster: A 90-Day Plan for Coaching New Teachers* (San Francisco, CA: Jossey-Bass).

Baum, L. Frank (1917). *The Lost Princess of Oz*, Project Gutenberg ebook edn (Chicago: The Reilly & Lee Co.). Available at: http://www.gutenberg.org/files/24459/24459-h/24459-h.htm.

Benton, T. and T. Gallacher (2018). Is Comparative Judgement Just a Quick Form of Multiple Marking? *Research Matters*, 22 (Autumn): 22–28. Available at: https://www.cambridgeassessment.org.uk/Images/514987-is-comparative-judgement-just-a-quick-form-of-multiple-marking-.pdf.

Benyohai, M. (2018). The Difference Between Measuring Progress and Attainment, *Medium* [blog] (7 June). Available at: https://medium.com/@mrbenyohai/the-difference-between-measuring-progress-and-attainment-7269a41cdd8.

Benyohai, M. (2019). Principles and Practices: Is There a Difference and Should We Care? *Medium* [blog] (20 August). Available at: https://medium.com/@mrbenyohai/principles-and-practices-9561a2999ffb.

Berne, E. (1961). *Transactional Analysis in Psychotherapy* (New York: Grove Press).

Buck, A. (2018). Difficult Conversations, *Buck's Fizz* [blog] (1 August). Available at: https://andybuckblog.wordpress.com/2018/08/01/difficult-conversations/.

Campbell, D. T. (1979). Assessing the Impact of Planned Social Change, *Evaluation and Program Planning*, 2(1): 67–90.

Cherry, K. (2020). The Affect Heuristic and Decision Making, *Verywell Mind* [blog] (7 May). Available at: https://www.verywellmind.com/what-is-the-affect-heuristic-2795028.

Clear, J. (n.d.). How to Be More Productive and Eliminate Time Wasting Activities by Using the 'Eisenhower Box', *JamesClear.com* [blog]. Available at: https://jamesclear.com/eisenhower-box.

Coe, R. (2013). *Improving Education: A Triumph of Hope over Experience*. Inaugural Lecture of Professor Robert Coe, Director of CEM and Professor of Education at the School of Education, Durham University, 19 June. Available at: http://www.cem.org/attachments/publications/ImprovingEducation2013.pdf.

Coe, R. (2018). Why Assessment May Tell You Less Than You Think – Part I, *CEM Blog* [blog] (21 November). Available at: https://www.cem.org/blog/why-assessment-may-tell-you-less-than-you-think-part-1.

Department for Education (2013). *History Programmes of Study: Key Stage 3 – National Curriculum in England*. Ref: DFE-00194-2013. Available at: https://assets.publishing.service.gov.uk/government/uploads/system/uploads/attachment_data/file/239075/SECONDARY_national_curriculum_-_History.pdf.

Department for Education (2019). GCSE results ('Attainment 8') (22 August). Available at: https://www.ethnicity-facts-figures.service.gov.uk/education-skills-and-training/11-to-16-years-old/gcse-results-attainment-8-for-children-aged-14-to-16-key-stage-4/latest#by-ethnicity.

Dickens, J. (2016). 'Gaming' Row Flares Up Again over Pixl Club's Advice for Schools to Use Three-Day ICT 'GCSE', *Schools Week* (22 March). Available at: https://schoolsweek.co.uk/gaming-row-flares-up-again-over-pixl-clubs-advice-for-schools-to-use-three-day-ict-gcse/.

Franklin, B. (1916). *Autobiography of Benjamin Franklin*, Project Gutenberg ebook edn (New York: Henry Holt and Company). Available at: https://www.gutenberg.org/files/20203/20203-h/20203-h.htm.

Gardner, D. P. et al. (1983). *A Nation at Risk: The Imperative for Education Reform* (Washington, DC: The National Commission on Excellence in Education). Available at: https://files.eric.ed.gov/fulltext/ED226006.pdf.

Garon-Carrier, G., M. Boivin, F. Guay, Y. Kovas, G. Dionne, J. P. Lemelin, J. R. Séguin, F. Vitaro and R. E. Tremblay (2016). Intrinsic Motivation and Achievement in Mathematics in Elementary School: A Longitudinal Investigation of their Association, *Child Development*, 87(1): 165–175.

Granger, C. (2008). Rasch Analysis Is Important to Understand and Use for Measurement, *Rasch Measurement Transactions*, 21(3): 1122–1123. Available at: https://www.rasch.org/rmt/rmt213d.htm.

Haidt, J. (2007). *The Happiness Hypothesis: Putting Ancient Wisdom to the Test of Modern Science* (London: Arrow).

Haidt, J., J. Patrick Seder and S. Kesebir (2008). Hive Psychology, Happiness, and Public Policy, *Journal of Legal Studies*, 37(2): 113–156.

Hays, B. (2018). First Came Homo Sapiens, Then Came the Modern Brain, *United Press International* (25 January). Available at: https://www.upi.com/Science_News/2018/01/25/First-came-Homo-sapiens-then-came-the-modern-brain/6111516907001/.

Heath, C. and D. Heath (2011). *Switch: How to Change Things When Change Is Hard* (New York: Random House Business Books).

Jecker, J. and D. Landy (1969). Liking a Person As a Function of Doing Him a Favour, *Human Relations*, 22(4): 371–378.

Kennedy, J. (1995). Debiasing the Curse of Knowledge in Audit Judgment, *The Accounting Review*, 70(2): 249–273.

Kennedy, M. M. (2019). How We Learn About Teacher Learning, *Review of Research in Education*, 43(1): 138–162. Available at: https://journals.sagepub.com/doi/pdf/10.3102/0091732X19838970.

Kirschner, P. A., J. Sweller and R. E. Clark (2006). Why Minimal Guidance During Instruction Does Not Work: An Analysis of the Failure of Constructivist, Discovery, Problem-Based, Experiential, and Inquiry-Based Teaching, *Educational Psychologist*, 41(2): 75–86.

Kishimi, I. and F. Koga (2013). *The Courage to Be Disliked: How to Free Yourself, Change Your Life and Achieve Real Happiness* (Sydney: Allen & Unwin).

Kraft, M. A. and J. P. Papay (2014). Can Professional Environments in Schools Promote Teacher Development? Explaining Heterogeneity in Returns to Teaching Experience, *Educational Effectiveness and Policy Analysis*, 36(4): 476–500.

Langer, E. J., A. Blank and B. Chanowitz (1978). The Mindlessness of Ostensibly Thoughtful Action: The Role of 'Placebic' Information in Interpersonal Interaction, *Journal of Personality and Social Psychology*, 36(6): 635–642.

Lemov, D. (2015). *Teach Like a Champion 2.0: 62 Techniques That Put Students on the Path to College* (San Francisco, CA: Jossey-Bass).

Miller, G. A. (1956). The Magical Number Seven, Plus or Minus Two: Some Limits on Our Capacity for Processing Information, *Psychological Review*, 63(2): 81–97.

Muller, J. Z. (2018). *The Tyranny of Metrics* (Princeton: Princeton University Press).

National Research Council (1994). *Learning, Remembering, Believing: Enhancing Human Performance*, eds D. Druckman and R. Bjork (Washington, DC: The National Academies Press).

Nebel, C. (2020). Learning 'Useless' Things in School is (Usually) NOT Useless, *The Learning Scientists* [blog] (7 February). Available at: https://www.learningscientists.org/blog/2020/2/7-1.

Nuthall, G. (2007). *The Hidden Lives of Learners* (Wellington: NZCER Press).

Nye, P. (2018). Some MATs Look to Have Been Hit Hard by the Withdrawal of ECDL, *FFT Education Datalab* (16 November). Available at: https://ffteducationdatalab.org.uk/2018/11/some-mats-look-to-have-been-hit-hard-by-the-withdrawal-of-ecdl/.

O'Neil, C. (2016). *Weapons of Math Destruction: How Big Data Increases Inequality and Threatens Democracy* (New York: Penguin Random House).

Raichura, P. (2019). Clear Teacher Explanations 1: Examples and Non-Examples, *Bunsen Blue* [blog] (20 October). Available at: https://bunsenblue.wordpress.com/2019/10/20/clear-teacher-explanations-i-examples-non-examples/.

Rawls, J. (1971). *A Theory of Justice* (Cambridge, MA: The Belknap Press).

Rees, T. and J. Barker (2020). 2020: A New Perspective for School Leadership? *Impact: Journal of the Chartered College of Teaching*, 9: 46–47.

Rees, T. and J. Barker (2020). Expert School Leadership: What Is It and How Might We Get More of It? [video], *researchED Home* (16 May). Available at: https://www.youtube.com/watch?v=g5c6a9kw-3E&t=28s.

Reif, F. (2008). *Applying Cognitive Science to Education: Thinking and Learning in Scientific and Other Complex Domains* (Cambridge, MA: The MIT Press).

Rhead, S., B. Black and A. Pinot de Moira (2018). *Marking Consistency Metrics: An Update*. Ref: Ofqual/18/6449/2 (Coventry: Ofqual). Available at: https://assets.publishing.service.gov.uk/government/uploads/system/uploads/attachment_data/file/759207/Marking_consistency_metrics_-_an_update_-_FINAL64492.pdf.

Rittel, H. W. J. and M. M. Webber (1973). Dilemmas in a General Theory of Planning, *Policy Sciences*, 4: 155–169.

Robinson, C. D., J. Gallus, M. G. Lee and T. Rogers (2019). The Demotivating Effect (and Unintended Message) of Awards, *Organizational Behavior and Human Decision Processes*. DOI: 10.1016/j.obhdp.2019.03.006. Available at: https://scholar.harvard.edu/files/todd_rogers/files/the_demotivating_effect_and_unintended_message_of_awards_vf_01.pdf.

Rosenshine, B. (2012). Principles of Instruction: Research Based Strategies That All Teachers Should Know, *American Educator* (Spring): 12–19, 39. Available at: https://www.aft.org/sites/default/files/periodicals/Rosenshine.pdf.

Scott, K. (2017). *Radical Candor: How to Get What You Want by Saying What You Mean* (New York: Macmillan).

Scott, K. (2019). *Radical Candor: How to Get What You Want by Saying What You Mean*, revised edn (London: Pan Macmillan).

Sivers, D. (2010). First Follower: Leadership Lessons from a Dancing Guy, *Derek Sivers* [blog] (2 November). Available at: https://sivers.org/ff.

Stokes, L., H. Rolfe, N. Hudson Sharp and S. Stevens (2015). *A Compendium of Evidence on Ethnic Minority Resilience to the Effects of Deprivation on Attainment: Research Report*. Ref: DFE-RR439A (London: Department for Education). Available at: https://assets.publishing.service.gov.uk/government/uploads/system/uploads/attachment_data/file/439861/RR439A-Ethnic_minorities_and_attainment_the_effects_of_poverty.pdf.

Stone, D. and S. Heen (2015). *Thanks for the Feedback: The Science and Art of Receiving Feedback Well* (New York: Penguin).

Sweller, J. (2011). Cognitive Load Theory. In J. P. Mestre and B. H. Ross (eds), *The Psychology of Learning and Motivation: Volume 55. The Psychology of Learning and Motivation: Cognition in Education* (Cambridge, MA: Elsevier Academic Press), pp. 37–76.

Taleb, N. N. (2018). What Do I Mean by Skin in the Game? My Own Version, *Medium* (5 March). Available at: https://medium.com/incerto/what-do-i-mean-by-skin-in-the-game-my-own-version-cc858dc73260.

Tan, K. (2016). Billionaire Jack Ma Teaches You How to Be Successful in Life and Business, *LinkedIn* (8 February). Available at: https://www.linkedin.com/pulse/billionaire-jack-ma-teaches-you-how-successful-life-business-tan.

United Nations Office on Drugs and Crime (2007). *Leader's Guide: Cognitive Behavioural and Relapse Prevention Strategies*, Treatnet Training Volume B, Module 3. Available at: https://www.unodc.org/ddt-training/treatment/VOLUME%20B/Volume%20B%20-%20Module%203/1.Leaders%20Guide/Presentation%20-%20VolB_M3.pdf.

Wiliam, D. (2019). Dylan Wiliam: Teaching Not a Research-Based Profession, *TES* (30 May). Available at: https://www.tes.com/news/dylan-wiliam-teaching-not-research-based-profession.

Wiliam, D. (2010). What Counts as Evidence of Educational Achievement? The Role of Constructs in the Pursuit of Equity in Assessment, *Review of Research in Education*, 34(1): 254–284.

Willingham, D. T. (2004). Ask the Cognitive Scientist: The Privileged Status of Story, *The American Educator* (summer). Available at: https://www.aft.org/periodical/american-educator/summer-2004/ask-cognitive-scientist.

Willingham, D. T. (2009). *Why Don't Students Like School? A Cognitive Scientist Answers Questions About How the Mind Works and What It Means for the Classroom* (San Francisco, CA: Jossey-Bass).

Willingham, D. T. (2016). On Metaphor, Memory, and John King, *Daniel Willingham – Science & Education* [blog] (18 April). Available at: http://www.danielwillingham.com/daniel-willingham-science-and-education-blog/on-metaphor-memory-and-john-king.

Worth, J. and J. Van den Brande (2020). *Teacher Autonomy: How Does It Relate to Job Satisfaction and Retention?* (Slough: National Foundation for Educational Research). Available at: https://tdtrust.org/wp-content/uploads/2020/01/teacher_autonomy_how_does_it_relate_to_job_satisfaction_and_retention.pdf.

Young, M. and J. Muller (2010). Three Educational Scenarios for the Future: Lessons from the Sociology of Knowledge, *European Journal of Education*, 45(1): 11–27. DOI: 10.1111/j.1465-3435.2009.01413.x.